ALL ABOUT
THE LABRADOR
◆
RETRIEVER

Robert J. Berndt
Richard L. Myers

Alpine
Blue Ribbon Books
Loveland, Colorado

ALL ABOUT THE LABRADOR RETRIEVER
Copyright ©2003 by Robert J. Berndt and Richard L. Myers.

Library of Congress Cataloging-in-Publication Data

Berndt, Robert J.
    All about the Labrador retriever / Robert J. Berndt, Richard L. Myers.
        p. cm.
    Rev. ed. of: The Labrador retriever. 1996.
    Includes bibliographical references (p.).
    ISBN 1-57779-042-1
        1. Labrador retriever. I. Myers, Richard L., 1939- II. Berndt, Robert J. Labrador retriever. III. Title.

SF429.L3B47 2003
636.752'7--dc21   2003050328

This book is available at special quantity discounts for breeders and for club promotions, premiums, or educational use. Write for details.

The information contained in this book is complete and accurate to the best of our knowledge. All recommendations are made without guarantee on the part of the author or Alpine Publications, Inc. The author and publisher disclaim any liability with the use of this information.

Design and layout: Laura Newport
Copyediting: Dianne Nelson

Front Cover Photos: (Left) Ch. Coalcreek's Gimme a Break owned by George and Lillian Knobloch; (Right) Top to bottom: Diamond R Rowdy Renegade, M.H., owned by P. Rothing; Ch. Kupros Sparctacus owned by Lorraine Robbenhaar-Taylor; Courtesy Erik Bergishagen, photo by Phoebe.
Back Cover Photo: Killingworth's Sadie, owned by Killingworth Labrador Retrievers.

First printing: June 2003

1 2 3 4 5 6 7 8 9 0

Printed in the United States of America.

Table of Contents

Preface   vii

The Labrador Retriever Personality   1

History of the Labrador Retriever   9

The Labrador Retriever Standard   15

Selecting a Labrador Retriever Puppy   23

Raising the Labrador Retriever   29

Manners for Your Labrador Retriever   35

Canine Health Conditions   43

Conditioning Your Labrador Retriever   55

Field Trials and Hunting Tests   61

Training the Labrador Retriever for the Field   73

Show Competition for the Labrador Retriever 93

The Versatile Labrador Retriever   105

Breeding and Whelping   117

Labrador Retrievers in the United States   127

Labrador Retrievers in Other Countries   143

Labrador Retriever Hall of Fame   151

Authors Richard L. Myers, left, and Robert J. Berndt, right.

About the Authors

Robert J. Berndt is an all-breed judge who has been active in both specialty and all-breed clubs. He was a delegate to the American Kennel Club, where he served on the Board of Directors and as Chairman of that Board.

He has received the Certificate with Honors in judging from the Canine Institute in London, England. He has authored books on several different breeds of dogs, a book on grooming and showing toy dogs, and two books published in 2001: *The Science and Techniques of Judging Dogs* and the *Judge's Handbook of Breed Standard Analysis*. He has also served on the Board of Directors of a college of veterinary medicine.

In his nondog life, Dr. Berndt was a professor and university administrator. He served as a paramedic coordinator for EMS and is a private pilot.

Richard L. Myers has been competitively involved with dogs for more than thirty years. He has shown Beagles, field-trialed both Labrador Retrievers and Beagles, and judged field trials for both breeds. He is frequently asked to demonstrate the retrieving and handling skills of Labrador Retrievers at a variety of social and community events. He is an avid duck and upland game hunter who has used Labrador Retrievers for hunting throughout the Midwest and South.

Dr. Myers received his doctorate in microbiology from the University of Oklahoma and has spent his entire career as a professor teaching microbiology and immunology. A considerable portion of his teaching career was spent as department head. He conducts an active research program and has published numerous papers in scientific journals. His book titled *Immunology: A Laboratory Manual* is widely used at major universities.

These two authors also teamed up to write *The Labrador Retriever*, an earlier work on this same topic published by Denlinger Publishing, Ltd. in 1983.

Acknowledgements

We would like to express our appreciation to all of the breeders who contributed their special knowledge about the breed and to everyone who submitted photographs. A sincere effort was made to represent kennels from all parts of the country.

A special thanks to Mrs. John Ippensen of Sunnybrook Acres Kennels for her reading and critique of the manuscript.

Preface

This book is a manual for new owners of a Labrador Retriever. Information is presented for owners of a companion dog as well as for those who might be interested in bench competition, field training, or field trials.

The goals that were expressed for our earlier book, *The Labrador Retriever* remain the same, but the information has been completely updated and an additional chapter has been added to reflect the new ways in which the versatility of the Labrador Retriever is being realized. The Breed Standard has been revised by the parent club, the Labrador Retriever Club, Inc., and new dogs have established their own records in the field and on the bench. The photographs in this edition will reflect the winning trends of today.

Robert J. Berndt and *Richard L. Myers*

Ch. Kupros Sperctacus owned by Lorraine Robbenhaar-Taylor. Photo © Kent and Donna Dannen.

THE LABRADOR RETRIEVER PERSONALITY

The Labrador Retriever is the true all-purpose dog. He is a hunting dog, an obedience dog, a working dog, and an ideal family companion. He is large enough and substantial enough to withstand the wear and tear of a family of children and even-tempered enough so that he will become neither irritable nor mean. His usual method of behavior when he is worn out from excessive play is to retreat to a peaceful corner to nap and to catch his breath. Frequently, the children follow him and end up using him as a pillow for their own nap. He basks in the love and affection of his young owners.

James A. Michener, one of America's favorite authors for more than half a century, has studied and written about various aspects of the history and culture of the United States. Michener demonstrates a great love for the Labrador Retriever and a thorough understanding of the breed in his best-selling novel, *Chesapeake*. The Labrador Retriever plays a significant role in this book in the action that occurred from the 1880s to the present day.

The Chesapeake Bay Retriever was the native-bred dog of the bay area and the favorite hunting dog for waterfowl because of his high resistance to the chilling waters of the bay. With the growth of the shellfish industry at the end of the nineteenth century and the need for ice for long-distance shipments, the ice banks of Labrador became an important resource. As ice was shipped from Labrador to the Chesapeake Bay communities, a regular commerce was established. It was not difficult to understand that sooner or later the Labrador Retriever would be introduced into the Chesapeake Bay region because of certain similarities in the hunting practices. The people of Labrador hunted fewer marshy regions than the hunters of the Chesapeake but felt that their dogs could easily compete with the Chesapeake Bay Retriever.

The competition between owners of the two breeds, and between individual dogs of each breed as they were field tested together, gives James Michener an opportunity to demonstrate his deep understanding of the Labrador Retriever. He presents a truly heroic picture of a loyal dog that works devotedly for his master. He is a loving fireside companion that affectionately follows his master through chilling waters in the true spirit of the hunt. He is an eager dog that works hard to control his enthusiasm when the time for retrieving the bird approaches.

According to James Michener, the rivalry between owners of the Chesapeake Bay Retriever and the Labrador Retriever is so keen that when a newcomer moves into one of the communities of the eastern shore of Chesapeake Bay, he is immediately asked the simple question, "Chesapeake or Labrador?" His future associations are immediately established by his answer.

The only possible drawback to a Labrador Retriever is his size. He is just too big for small apartments. He also needs yard space to get the proper amount of exercise if he is to maintain himself in the proper condition. If he does not get an opportunity to exercise properly, he will become overweight and lazy. Because jogging is so much in vogue at present, it does give you an opportunity to exercise your dog by taking him on a daily jog for a mile or two. It is beneficial for both you and your dog.

The Labrador Retriever is easy to train. He is a ready learner and is almost always happy during training sessions when they are presented as a part of the regular routine of his life. If the sessions become too monotonous and too long, the dog, just like you, will lose interest and will not work well. A break in training with a day or two off will usually bring him back to full eagerness.

The distinguished author James A. Michener with (left to right) FC Sassy Sioux of Tukwila, C.D., FC Zoe, and FC Zipper's Dapper Sapper. These three field champions belong to Mr. Michener's friend, Mr. Don Gearheart.

The Labrador Retriever is an easy and willing learner. Patterns can be taught with a minimum of presentation, and practice usually hones the exercise to a fine edge. Training can be started as early as six weeks of age. When you start this early, however, make it into a game and keep the sessions short to accommodate the puppy's attention span. This will prevent boredom and resentment. Short but regularly scheduled training sessions are best.

As the Labrador Retriever ages and matures, training sessions can become longer and more demanding. Labradors seem to relish the challenge of each new phase of the training routines and actively work to learn it in an effort to please you. The eagerness with which he approaches his work is always intriguing to any bystander who happens to come upon a training session.

The flexibility of the Labrador Retriever is one of his strong qualities and one that makes him a good family companion. He adjusts easily and is willing to accept new challenges, opportunities, and surroundings without becoming upset. He is a calm and moderate being in almost all aspects of his life.

The Labrador Retriever does enjoy being pampered and even enjoys being spoiled—just as do his human counterparts. He will respond with love and devotion when he receives special attention. He enjoys sitting at your feet frequently with his head resting directly on your feet. He will sleep there contentedly, but with the least stir, he is up and ready for whatever action you have planned for him. During the warmer months, he may pick as a resting place a doorway where there is a breeze. This also gives him the opportunity to watch over special areas of activity in the house and prevent anyone from sneaking out without taking him along.

Every Labrador Retriever, because of his size, must have at least a minimum of obedience training. He is just too large to be allowed to misbehave, even though he

Every Lab needs at least some basic obedience training. This one is competing in a "Rally" obedience class. Photo © Judith Strom.

Labrador puppies are usually calm and accepting and make great pets. Photo © Robert and Eunice Pearcy.

might be in a playful mood. Guests in a home do not like to be jumped on or bumped by anyone's cute little Rover—and with this particular breed, Rover is definitely not little. The dog must be taught not to jump, to come when called, to stay at heel, and to sit when ordered to do so. This is the minimum level of acceptable behavior that can be expected of a house dog. Dogs that are to be worked for the field or for shows will need additional

A Labrador puppy will want to go everywhere with you. Be sure he is wearing a collar. Photo © Kent and Donna Dannen.

Two of the things Labradors love most: retrieving and swimming. Photo © Karen Hudson.

training, because their standards of behavior are more demanding.

Complete obedience training is not necessary, although it can be accomplished easily with the Labrador Retriever. Each year, many Labrador Retriever owners elect to take their dogs through obedience training. This is not popular with every owner because of the amount of work and time it requires. Many Labrador Retrievers have earned the title of Companion Dog (CD), Companion Dog Excellent (CDX), Utility Dog (UD), Obedience Trial Champion (OTCh.), Tracking Dog (TD), and Tracking Dog Excellent (TDX). Numerous Labrador Retrievers have become a Field Trial Champion (FC), an Amateur Field Trial Champion (AFC), a Junior Hunter (JH), a Senior Hunter (SH), or a Master Hunter (MH). There are also the agility titles of Agility Novice (NA), Agility Open (OA), and Agility Excellent (AX).

One example of a well-trained Labrador Retriever was seen in a show in the Midwest. A young male had been shown by a handler and had gone Winners Dog. The handler had subsequently handled another dog that had won Best of Breed, and he was in the ring having this dog's picture taken. The owner was holding the Winners Dog at ringside, waiting for his turn to have his picture taken. To get the attention of the Best-of-Breed dog being photographed, the photographer slapped a folded newspaper on the floor and tossed it across the ring. The Winners Dog standing outside the ring was being trained at home to retrieve dummies, and, seeing this dummylike object fly across the ring, he broke loose from his owner, leaped the fence around the ring, and retrieved the newspaper. He leaped back across the fence and finished correctly in front of his owner, who was still standing there with a surprised look on his face.

Occasionally, a Labrador Retriever will become bored while being shown in conformation, just as do dogs of many other breeds. You either stop showing your dog for a while or try to find ring techniques that will bring a new excitement in the ring. One owner discovered that her bitch became very animated out in the field when told to "Find the bird." She decided to try this in the ring and discovered, to her great surprise, that it worked very well. When the judge would come down the line, the owner would say, "Find the bird," and the bitch would lean forward, raise her head, and stretch her neck in an effort to find a bird up high somewhere. At one of the shows that was being held in a fairgrounds arena building, some birds had made a nest in the rafters. It was directly behind the judge as he came down the line examining each dog. There were young birds in the nest, and they were chirping continuously. The bitch was very intent, frozen in a perfect pose, straining to see the birds. Her efforts were well rewarded that day, for she won the major.

The outgoing personality of the Labrador Retriever has always made him a keen competitor in whatever he undertakes. One example of this is seen in the black five-year-old Labrador Retriever bitch Belmond, owned by police officer Bob Cox of Des Moines, Iowa. Belmont tied for first place in the World Final of the Cycle Catch and Fetch competition sponsored by the Gaines Dog Research Center in White Plains, New York. The Catch and Fetch is a canine version of the Frisbee disc game.

One year, the top ten winners of the Ken-L Ration Dog Hero of the Year award included one Labrador Retriever and one part Labrador Retriever. One recipient was Bo, a Labrador owned by Mr. and Mrs. Rob Roberts of Glenwood Springs, Colorado. While boating on the Colorado River, the Roberts's boat had overturned and Mrs. Roberts had been trapped under the boat. Bo had dived under the boat, pulled Mrs. Roberts out by the hair, and safely towed her to shore.

Bandit is a part Labrador Retriever owned by Mr. and Mrs. Michael Woods of Pell Lake, Wisconsin. One day while Mr. Woods had been sleeping, the house had caught fire and Bandit had awakened his master by licking his face. Because the smoke was so thick, Mr. Woods had been unable to find his way to safety. Bandit had stayed with his master and guided him to safety through the smoke-filled rooms.

There seems to be no limit to what a Labrador Retriever can be taught to do. A friend in the Biology Department at a Midwestern university recently complained to me that his students were hav-

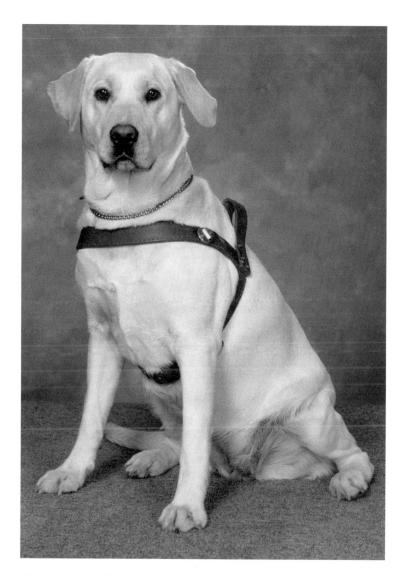

Their steady, dependable disposition makes Labrador Retrievers a favorite as seeing eye dogs. Photo courtesy of Guiding Eyes for the Blind, Inc.

ing difficulty finding box turtles that were a major part of an ecological research program conducted for the Conservation Department. He explained that even on a good day, he could find no more than two or three turtles in a forty-acre tract of conservation land. I suggested that my Labrador Retriever might help, and, after looking puzzled for a moment, he began to laugh.

That evening I simply indicated to my Lab what I would like for him to do by holding a box turtle in front of him and saying, "Fetch." He eagerly but gently took the turtle and sat beside me awaiting

Labradors are active dogs that need an outlet for their energy and they are keen competitors in whatever dog sport they compete in.

Top Right: Danielle Champagne, C.D.X., picks out the article with her owner's scent in the scent discrimination exercise at a Utility obedience competition.

This black Lab is learning to grab the ball in a flyball competition, and another dog on the team races toward the finish line.

"Sonya" jumps through a tire, and "Meggie" clears a jump in agility class. Photos © Judith Strom.

the next command. Next, I placed the turtle in tall grass and walked the dog to the area, repeating the command, "Dead bird." The command means to search the area for a fallen bird, but in this case the dog knew that we were now hunting turtles. He found the turtle within seconds and with that understood our new strategy. The next day we accompanied the doubting professor and his group of graduate students to their study area. Of course there were jokes about the "Turtle-dog" and "Professor Turtle," but the comments quickly faded when I commanded, "Dead bird," and my dog went to work. He began to collect turtles at a staggering pace, and within less than an hour he had retrieved thirty-eight box turtles. "Enough" was the first response from the professor and that was quickly followed by, "Great dog you have there." From that time on, my Lab was a frequent companion (and coworker) of his group, and the results of the study led to a master's thesis and two publications in major journals.

The next September, a hunting buddy asked if he could use that same dog while we were hunting doves over a grain field. I gladly agreed, because I wanted to work with a young dog that I had recently purchased. I could see my friend and dog across the field and was pleased to see him make a very nice left-to-right shot on a fast-moving dove. The dove fell behind him and to the right in a field of very tall prairie grass. He sent my dog, and after a long hunt, I could see the dog coming back with his prize. Later, back at the truck, my friend remarked that I sure have a fine hunting dog, and that he is a joy to work and watch but that "he seems to have a small problem." I was concerned because my friend is a fine judge of good dog work, so I asked for an explanation. My friend said, "He couldn't find one of the doves, so he brought me a box turtle."

Any Labrador Retriever breeder or owner is a storehouse of tales about his dogs. When breeders get together, it is almost like playing "Can You Top This?"

Labradors are also popular as Canine Companions. This dog wears the coat that identifies him as a dog in training for Canine Companions for independence. Photo © Judith Strom.

Above all else, the Labrador is a retriever! Here Ch. Tabatha's Dodena of Franklin, C.D., T.D., W.C. is shown "doing what comes naturally." Photo © Carol A Heidl.

The Stud Dog Class at the American Labrador Retriever Club National Specialty in 1992. Left to right, Ch. Hennings Mills Master Blend and his two sons, Am. Can. Ch. Flying Cloud's Tai Pan and Ch. Willcare's Masterpiece. Master Blend is owned by Charlotte Veneziano. Photo © Sandy Tatham.

Each tries to outdo the other with an even more outlandish tale to prove that his dogs are smarter than all others. You usually do not even have to ask in order to hear a new story, for often it will be told before an invitation is extended.

In spite of the truthfulness or inventiveness of the stories, the Labrador Retriever is a faithful and lifelong friend. His true value far exceeds whatever monetary figure can be put on him as a great show dog, a top hunter, or a prepotent sire. His values lie in the pleasure and friendship he offers to his owners. This is, of course, a highly subjective valuation, but it is one that almost any owner is willing to defend.

HISTORY OF THE LABRADOR RETRIEVER

While it is difficult, if not impossible, to establish a precise date for the emergence of an individual breed that has a long history, this is not true for a breed that was created in recent times. Breeds that have been developed in the last 100 to 200 years are relatively easy to trace because of the interest of breeders in maintaining breeding records in an effort to improve the breed. This, however, is not the case with the ancient breeds that have gone through centuries of evolution, resulting in the purebred dogs that exist today. Few, if any, early records exist to substantiate the first phases of development of these long-established breeds.

The modern Labrador Retriever has a history of perhaps 150 years. While there were retrieving dogs prior to this date, the precise type did not exist. There is evidence of the earlier existence of the retriever-type dog in both literature and art. Paintings and sculptures have frequently served to establish historical authenticity in the absence of written proof.

Many dogs that are today associated with the northern countries trace their origin back to central Europe. This seems only natural, because dogs living in a wild or semidomesticated state would find the climate of central Europe more amenable to that of some other areas and would, therefore, be able to survive and multiply.

When these same dogs were transported to northern climates, they would need some help and protection from man in order to survive.

Modern domestic dogs all trace back to four different categories in determining their origin: the Dingo group, the northern group, the Greyhound group, and the Mastiff group. The Labrador Retriever belongs with those dogs classified in the Mastiff group (*Molossoides*). Others included in this group are the Newfoundland, the Doberman Pinscher, the Schnauzer, the Bulldog, the Saint Bernard, the French Bulldog, the Chihuahua, and the Pug.

An etching by Dianne Ziessow of Ch. Golden Chance of Franklin, an influential Retriever in the past.

Labrador is the eastern most province of Canada. It is bordered on the west and the south by Quebec and on the east by the Atlantic Ocean. It is just north of the Island of Newfoundland.

Small domesticated hunting dogs appeared centuries before the birth of Christ in the lands at the eastern end of the Mediterranean Sea. This is testified to by the early Greek writings of Xenephon in the fourth century B.C. In *Cynegeticus*, a treatise on the hunting of hare, wild boar, and deer, Xenephon refers to the small hunting dogs of the period.

References to these small dogs were common in both Greek and Roman literature for several centuries. The Romans divided dogs into six different categories according to their value to man. These divisions were fighting dogs *(Pugnacaes),* scent dogs *(Nares Sagaces),* coursing sight dogs *(Pedibus Celeres),* hunting dogs *(Venatici),* herding dogs *(Pastorales),* and house dogs *(Villatici).* The early ancestors of the Labrador Retriever would have come from the hunting-herding dogs.

These hunting dogs were probably carried north across Europe by traveling huntsmen. The small dogs were used on small game, allowing the larger dogs to pursue large animals such as wild boar, deer, and bear.

Authorities agree that the immediate ancestors for the modern Labrador Retriever came from the Labrador-Ungave and Newfoundland regions of Canada. Agreement seems to end there, for how the original dogs reached those areas is open to much speculation. One of the theories that seems to have some validity is that the original dogs were brought from Europe. Early ships' logs do not make any mention of native New World dogs in these areas of Canada. This does add an element of veracity to the theory of the ancestors having been imported from Europe.

One of the possibilities is that the sixteenth-century Breton cod fishermen from France brought with them their *Braque Francais.* This hunting-type dog had some of the characteristics of the modern pointer and is considered by many as the common ancestor for most spaniels and retrievers. This *Braque* dog had a somewhat large-sized head for his body. He did have an excellent nose and an outstanding temperament.

References also have been made to the visits of the English fishing boats to these regions in the sixteenth century. Newfoundland was a colony of England, and trade most certainly occurred between the colony and the mother country. There is also the suggestion that a Mastiff-type dog from one of these boats mated with some of the wolves and thus started a new breed. Because there are no accurate records of such events from this period, you can speculate on your own as to which story makes the most sense.

As early as 1814, a Colonel Peter Hawker makes reference to a Newfoundland-type dog that he saw on one of his trips to the colony. The assumption at the time was that this retriever had been bred to add game and fowl to a diet of fish.

Travelers' reports from the 1820s refer to the retrievers seen along the coasts. These dogs were short haired and had smooth coats. They apparently had been bred for these qualities so that they would be able to work in the frigid waters and their coats would not absorb the water and become caked with ice.

Colonel Hawker refers to the Saint John's water dog in 1830. These dogs were used along the coast to retrieve fish as well as downed birds. Again there is mention of the short, water-repellent coat. About this same time, some of these dogs were taken back to England on the cod-fishing boats.

By the 1850s, different varieties of the breed were beginning to be noticed. They were referred to as the Newfoundland Retriever and the Saint John's Retriever. The latter was a smaller dog and one more suited to the small boats that were being used for duck hunting in the marshlands. A large dog would have been unmanageable in a small boat and would have caused great problems when springing from the light boat and even greater problems when trying to climb back in. He easily could have capsized the little boats. The larger dog would not have been as agile and probably would not have been as good of a swimmer, because he had a somewhat longer coat.

The breed began to die out during the last half of the nineteenth century, as did many other breeds that existed then. This was due to the passage of a law rather than to a lack of interest among dog owners. The government levied a rather oppressive tax on dogs, and, in an economy based on trade rather than on cash, the tax almost eliminated the entire dog population of Newfoundland.

At about the same time, a different type of law was passed in England. While it was different, it did bring the importation of dogs almost to a complete halt. A very rigid quarantine was imposed on all imported dogs. While the very rich and probably the very patient were still able to bring in outstanding dogs from abroad, the normal traffic in dogs slowed almost

L.WELLS.

"Billy," a St. John's or Lesser Labrador dog. From *Stonehenge on the Dog*, Second Edition, 1873.

Two current campions . . .
Ch. Highlands California Cooler, owned by G. Knobloch.

Ch. Highlands Madd Max, owned by G. Knobloch.

to the point of stopping. England today still has one of the most restrictive quarantine laws of any country in the world. With the opening of the Channel between England and France and the pressure of the European Common Market Community, England may have to revise its quarantine laws to accommodate the other countries.

The real development of the Labrador Retriever undoubtedly took place in England after these different but highly restrictive laws were passed. Hunters began

to experiment with crossbreeding in an effort to try to improve the retrieving qualities of the breed. Crosses were made with pointers and setters to modify size, or to improve the nose, or to add a note of calmness to the dog. Dogs bred in Scotland maintained a greater purity to the original type and thus kept a more Mastiff-type head.

The year 1887 seems to be when the breed finally took on a name of its own. The Earl of Malmesbury used the name "Labrador" in a letter he wrote, in which he discussed some of the dogs in his kennel. Shortly thereafter, the name "Labrador Retriever" was generally accepted by the breeders.

All of the original specimens of the breed were black, and no reference is made to a yellow until 1899. When yellows first appeared, they were sometimes called "goldens." This name, however, was eliminated later in order to avoid confusion with the Golden Retriever.

The Kennel Club of England recognized the breed in 1904. It was not until 1906, however, that a Labrador Retriever first ran in a trial. This dog was Mundin Single, and he was owned by A. Holland Hibbert.

Lord Knutsford was an active founder of the Labrador Club of England in 1916. It was at this time that the Standard of the breed was firmed up.

One of the most active English breeders, and the one person who undoubtedly did most for the breed between World War I and World War II, was the Countess Howe. While many dogs were exhibited under her kennel name "Banchory," she bought and showed many dogs that she did not breed. Her dedication to the breed was testified to by breeders across England. Her knowledge of the breed was acknowledged by her frequent judging assignments at Crufts. She had the distinction of being the first person to finish a dual-champion Labrador Retriever, Ch. Banchory Bolo, in 1919. Another of her great dual champions was Ch. Bramshow Bob, who went Best in Show at Crufts in both 1933 and 1934.

Three Labs from the mid-20th century . . .

Left: Ch. Dark Star of Franklin

Middle: Dark Star's full brother, Ch. Franklin's Troublemaker, was first in both Veteran's and Stud Dog Class at the 1960 National Specialty.

Right: Ch. Aldenholme's Robbieson, owned by Mrs. B. Barty-King. Photo by Brown.

During the period between the two world wars, a number of Labrador Retrievers were imported into the United States. The American Kennel Club (AKC) officially recognized the breed in 1931 and licensed the first Labrador Retriever trial in the country in the state of New York in the same year.

W. Averill Harriman was an early importer of the breed. He bred and showed the dogs under his Arden Kennel prefix. In 1935, the first American field trial champion was finished. This dog was Ch. Blind of Arden from the Harriman kennel.

Arden Kennel dates from the 1920s and was located in the eastern United States. In addition to breeding the first American field champion, the kennel also accounts for the three-time

NATIONAL AMATEUR CHAMPIONSHIP WINNERS, 1990-2002

1990 FC & AFC Candlewood's Super Tanker
1991 FC & AFC Cody's R. Dee
1992 FC & AFC Gusto's Lost Control
1993 FC & AFC M.D.'s Cotton Pick'N Cropper
1994 FC & AFC Lady Andrel's Nighthawk Lady
1995 FC & AFC Rugbyu's Coiwin Flight
1996 FC & AFC Candlewood's Bit O Bunny
1997 FC & AFC Fishtrap Calamity
1998 FC & AFC Hattie McBunn
1999 FC & NAFC Candlewood's Bit O Bunny
2000 FC & NAFC Ebonstar Lean Mac
2001 FC & AFC Candlewood's Ramblin Man
2002 FC & AFC Candlewood's Ramblin Man

NATIONAL OPEN RETRIEVER WINNERS 1990-2002

1990 FC & AFC Candlewood's Tanks A Lot
1991 NFC & AFC Candlewood's Tanks A Lot
1992 NFC & AFC Candlewood's Super Tanker
1993 NFC & AFC Candlewood's Tanks A Lot
1994 FC & AFC Lucille Double Or Nothin'
1995 FC & AFC M.D.'s Cotton Pick'N Cropper
1996 FC Storm's Riptide Star
1997 FC & AFC Lucyana's Fast Willie
1998 FC & AFC Abe's Ebony and Ivory
1999 FC & AFC Croppers River Water Black Teal
2000 FC Maxx's Surprise
2001 FC & AFC Eagle Ridge Rocket Sam
2002 FC & AFC Cashman's Fat Lady Zingin

THE LABRADOR RETRIEVER CLUB OF AMERICA
Best of Breed Winners

1990 Ch. Chelon's Firestorm
1991 Ch. Chocorua's Seabreeze
1992 Ch. Breezy's Whirlaway
1993 Ch. Tabatha's Dazzle
1994 Campbellcroft P.B. Max CD
1995 Ch. Hickory Ridge Gustav Mahler
1996 Ch. Chablais Myrtille
1997 Faunhaven's Sonny Boy
1998 Ch. Boradors Significant Brother
1999 Ch. Winterwind's Zeus
      Mach Two
2000 Ch. Sounder's Hear Me Roar
2001 Ch. Ruthless Blazing
      Brentley
2002 Ch. Lobuff's Turtle Dove

winner of the Nationals with Dual Ch. Shed of Arden. His dam was FC Decoy of Arden, who was a littermate of Blind. Other winners from this kennel were Dual Ch. Bengal of Arden, Dual Ch. Braes of Arden, Dual Ch. Gorse of Arden, and FC Tar of Arden.

Shed of Arden was purchased from the Harrimans by Mr. and Mrs. Paul Bakewell III of Missouri, who showed him to his outstanding record. He was a leading sire of the time. The Deercreek Kennel of the Bakewells dates from the 1930s. Winners carrying the kennel name include Dual Ch. Little Pierre of Deercreek, his son, Dual Ch. Matchmaker for Deercreek, FC Pickpocket of Deercreek, and FC Firelei of Deercreek.

The first dual champion in the United States was Michael of Glenmere, owned by Jerry Angle of Nebraska. Among the early multiple Best-in-Show winners are Ch. Earlsmoor Moor, Ch. Dark Star of Franklin, Eng./Am./Can.Ch. Sam of Blaircourt, and the record-setting Ch. Shamrock Acres Light Brigade.

The National Retriever Championship Stake and the National Amateur Championship Stake are trials run each year with entrants qualifying by placing in trials run during the calendar year. The dogs that qualify are, therefore, the very best of all dogs trialed, and the competition is stiff. To qualify for the National Open, a dog must have taken five championship points for a first place, plus two additional points in an Open or Limited All-Age class of an AKC Member or Licensed Trial. To qualify for the National Amateur, the dog must be handled by an amateur, have a first place that carries five points, and have two additional points acquired in an Amateur, Open, or Limited All-Age class of an AKC Member or Licensed Trial.

Past winners of these prestigious titles are listed to the left.

THE LABRADOR RETRIEVER STANDARD

Only purebred dogs are recognized by the American Kennel Club (AKC). The AKC promulgates rules and regulations for the breeding and showing of these purebred dogs and offers guidance to breeders.

Before obtaining recognition for a breed, the parent club must establish a Standard of Perfection. This Standard is a detailed description for that particular breed and can be used as a measuring device for evaluating the dogs of that breed. The Standard is the result of the efforts of the breeders who have sought the recognition of the AKC for their breed. Over a period of years, the AKC has acted as a semiofficial registering agency for all information. This includes litter registrations, records, studbooks, and other information pertinent to the development of the breed, such as the history and the evolution and the importing and exporting of individual dogs.

After a period of probation in which the consistency of the breed has been demonstrated, the AKC allows the breed to be exhibited in the Miscellaneous Class at dog shows. Following a period of time during which the judges have an opportunity to become familiar with the breed, and the exhibitors have an opportunity to demonstrate that there is sufficient interest, the breed is officially recognized and can be shown in regular breed and group competition. Dogs can also be entered in field trials and hunting tests.

When the breed is officially recognized, the Standard is formally accepted by the AKC. Judges and breeders use this official description in determining the quality of the dogs. Standards are, however, difficult documents to prepare and to interpret. Size and weight descriptions present no problems, but when adjectives appear in abundance, it is difficult to interpret the exact meaning of the writers. Because tastes change from time to time and new breeders become dominant and active in the breed clubs, Standards may be rewritten. Such evolutionary changes help to explain why pictures of breed winners of twenty or thirty years ago appear quite different from those of the winners today.

INTERPRETATION OF THE STANDARD

The Labrador Retriever is to be a short-coupled dog. Many Breed Standards call for short coupling, but in the case of the Labrador Retriever, the overall balance of the structure of the dog and the original purpose for which he was bred must be considered. A field dog must move over open ground for long periods of time and

THE AMERICAN KENNEL CLUB STANDARD FOR THE LABRADOR RETRIEVER

The following is the official Standard for the Labrador Retriever, which was revised by the Labrador Retriever Club, Inc. and approved by the AKC on March 31, 1994.

General Appearance

The Labrador Retriever is a strongly built medium-sized, short-coupled dog possessing a sound, athletic well-balanced conformation that enables it to function as a retrieving gun dog; the substance and soundness to hunt waterfowl or upland game for long hours under difficult conditions; the character and quality to win in the show ring; and the temperament to be a family companion. Physical features and mental characteristics should denote a dog bred to perform as an efficient Retriever of game with a stable temperament suitable for a variety of pursuits beyond the hunting environment.

The most distinguishing characteristics of the Labrador Retriever are its short, dense weather resistant coat; and "otter" tail; a clean-cut head with broad back skull and moderate stop; powerful jaws; and its "kind," friendly eyes, expressing character, intelligence and good temperament.

Above all, a Labrador Retriever must be well balanced, enabling it to move in the show ring or work in the field with little or no effort. The typical Labrador possesses style and quality without over refinement, and substance without lumber or cloddiness. The Labrador is bred primarily as a working gun dog; structure and soundness are of great importance.

Size, Proportion, and Substance

Size—The height at the withers for a dog is 22 1/2 to 24 1/2 inches; for a bitch is 21 1/2 to 23 1/2 inches. Any variance greater than 1/2 inch above or below these heights is a disqualification. Approximate weight of dogs and bitches in working condition: dogs 65 to 80 pounds; bitches 55 to 70 pounds.

The minimum height ranges set forth in the paragraph above shall not apply to dogs or bitches under twelve months of age.

Proportion—Short-coupled; length from the point of the shoulders to the point of the rump is equal to or slightly longer than the distance from the withers to the ground. Distance from the elbow to the ground should be equal to one-half of the height at the withers. The brisket should extend to the elbows, but not perceptibly deeper. The body must be of sufficient length to permit a straight, free and efficient stride; but the dog should never appear low and long or tall and leggy in outline.

Substance—Substance and bone proportionate to the overall dog. Light, "weedy" individuals are definitely incorrect; equally objectionable are cloddy lumbering specimens. Labrador Retrievers shall be shown in working condition well-muscled and without excess fat.

Head

Skull—The skull should be wide; well developed but without exaggeration. The skull and foreface should be on parallel planes and of approximately equal length. There should be a moderate stop—the brow slightly pronounced so that the skull is not absolutely in a straight line with the nose. The brow ridges aid in defining the stop. The head should be clean-cut and free from fleshy cheeks; the bony structure of the skull chiseled beneath the eye with no prominence in the cheek. The skull may show some median line; the occipital bone is not conspicuous in mature dogs. Lips should not be squared off or pendulous, but fall away in a curve toward the throat. A wedge-shaped head, or a head long and narrow in muzzle and back skull is incorrect as are massive, cheeky heads. The jaws are powerful and free from snippiness—the muzzle neither long and narrow nor short and stubby. Nose—The nose should be wide and the nostrils well-developed. The nose should be black on black or yellow dogs, and brown on chocolate. Nose color fading to a lighter shade is not a fault. A thoroughly pink nose or one lacking in any pigment is a disqualification. Teeth—The teeth should be strong and regular with a scissors bite; the lower teeth just behind, but touching the inner side of the upper incisors. A level bite is acceptable, but not desirable. Undershot, overshot, or misaligned teeth are serious faults. Full dentition is preferred. Missing molars or pre-molars are serious faults. Ears—The ears should hang moderately close to the head, set rather far back, and somewhat low on the skull; slightly above eye level. Ears should not be large and heavy, but in proportion with the skull and reach to the inside of the eye when pulled forward. Eyes—Kind, friendly eyes imparting good temperament, intelligence and alertness are a hallmark of the breed. They should be of medium size, set well apart, and neither protruding nor deep set. Eye color should be brown in black and yellow Labradors, and brown or hazel in chocolates. Black, or yellow eyes give a harsh expression and are undesirable. Small eyes, set close together or round prominent eyes are not typical of the breed. Eye rims are black in black and yellow Labradors; and brown in chocolates. Eye rims without pigmentation is a disqualification.

Neck, Topline, Body

Neck—The neck should be of proper length to allow the dog to retrieve game easily. It should be muscular and free from throatiness. The neck should rise strongly from the shoulders with a moderate arch. A short, thick neck or "ewe" neck is incorrect. *Topline*—The back is strong and the topline is level from the withers to the croup when standing or moving. However, the loin should show evidence of flexibility for athletic endeavor. *Body*—The Labrador should be short-coupled, with good spring of ribs tapering to a moderately wide chest. The Labrador should not be narrow chested; giving the appearance of hollowness between the front legs, nor should it have a wide spreading, bulldog-like front. Correct chest conformation will result in tapering between the front legs that allows unrestricted forelimb movement. Chest breadth that is either too wide or too narrow for efficient movement and stamina is incorrect. Slab-sided individuals are not typical of the breed; equally objectionable are rotund or barrel chested specimens. The underline is almost straight, with little or no tuck-up in mature animals. Loins should be short, wide and strong; extending to well developed, powerful hindquarters. When viewed from the side, the Labrador Retriever shows a well-developed, but not exaggerated forechest. *Tail*—The tail is a distinguishing feature of the breed. It should be very thick at the base, gradually tapering toward the tip, of medium length, and extending no longer than to the hock. The tail should be free from feathering and clothed thickly all round with the Labrador's short, dense coat, thus having the peculiar rounded appearance that has been described as "otter" tail. The tail should follow the topline in repose or when in motion. It may be carried gaily, but should not curl over the back. Extremely short tails or long thin tails are serious faults. The tail completes the balance of the Labrador by giving it a flowing line from the top of the head to the tip of the tail. Docking or otherwise altering the length or natural carriage of the tail is a disqualification.

Forequarters

Forequarters should be muscular, well coordinated and balanced with the hindquarters. *Shoulders*—The shoulders are well laid-back, long and sloping, forming an angle with the upper arm of approximately 90 degrees that permits the dog to move his forelegs in an easy manner with strong forward reach. Ideally, the length of the shoulder blade should equal the length of the upper arm. Straight shoulder blades, short upper arms or heavily muscled or loaded shoulders, all restricting free movement, are incorrect. *Front Legs*—When viewed from the front, the legs should be straight with good strong bone. Too much bone is as undesirable as too little bone, and short legged, heavy boned individuals are not typical of the breed. Viewed from the side, the elbows should be directly under the withers, and the front legs should be perpendicular to the ground and well under the body. The elbows should be close to the ribs without looseness. Tied-in elbows or being "out at the elbows" interfere with free movement and are serious faults. Pasterns should be strong and short and should slope slightly from the perpendicular line of the leg. Feet are strong and compact, with well-arched toes and well-developed pads. Dew claws may be removed. Splayed feet, hare feet, knuckling over, or feet turning in or out are serious faults.

Hindquarters

The Labrador's hind-quarters are broad, muscular and well-developed from the hip to the hock with well-turned stifles and strong short hocks. Viewed from the rear, the hind legs are straight and parallel. Viewed from the side, the angulation of the rear legs is in balance with the front. The hind legs are strongly boned, muscled with moderate angulation at the stifle, and powerful, clearly defined thighs. The stifle is strong and there is no slippage of the patellae while in motion or when standing. The hock joints are strong, well let down and do not slip or hyper-extend while in motion or when standing. Angulation of both stifle and hock joint is such as to achieve the optimal balance of drive and traction. When standing the rear toes are only slightly behind the point of the rump. Over angulation produces a sloping topline not typical of the breed. Feet are strong and compact, with well-arched toes and well-developed pads. Cow-hocks, spread-hocks, sickle hocks and over-angulation are serious defects and are to be faulted.

Coat

The coat is a distinctive feature of the Labrador Retriever. It should be short, straight and very dense, giving a fairly hard feeling to the hand. The Labrador should have a soft, weather-resistant undercoat that provides protection from water, cold and all types of ground cover. A slight wave down the back is permissible. Wooly coats, soft silky coats, and sparse slick coats are not typical of the breed, and should be severely penalized.

Color

The Labrador Retriever coat colors are black, yellow and chocolate. Any other color or a combination of colors is a disqualification. A small white spot on the chest is permissible, but not desirable. White hairs from aging or scarring are not to be misinterpreted as brindling. *Black*—Blacks are all black. A black with brindle markings or a black with tan markings is a disqualification. *Yellow*—Yellows may range in color from fox-red to light cream, with variations in shadings on the ears, back and underparts of the dog. *Chocolate*—Chocolates can vary in shade from light to dark chocolate. Chocolate with brindle or tan markings is a disqualification.

Disqualification

Movement of the Labrador Retriever should be free and effortless. When watching a dog move toward oneself, there should be no sign of elbows out. Rather, the elbows should be held neatly to the body with the legs not too close together. Moving straight forward without pacing or weaving, the legs should form straight lines, with all parts moving in the same plane. Upon viewing the dog from the rear, one should have the impression that the hind legs move as nearly as possible in a parallel line with the front legs. The hocks should do their full share of the work, flexing well, giving the appearance of power and strength. When viewed from the side, the shoulders should move freely and effortlessly, and the foreleg should reach forward close to the ground with extension. A short, choppy movement or high knee action indicates a straight shoulder; paddling indicates long, weak pasterns; and a short, stilted rear gait indicates a straight rear assembly; all are serious faults. Movement faults interfering with performance including weaving; side-winding; crossing over; high knee action; paddling; and short, choppy movement, should be severely penalized.

Temperament

True Labrador Retriever temperament is as much a hallmark of the breed is the "otter" tail. The ideal disposition is one of a kindly, outgoing, tractable nature; eager to please and non-aggressive towards man or animal. The Labrador has much that appeals to people; his gentle ways, intelligence and adaptability make him an ideal dog. Aggressiveness towards humans or other animals, or any evidence of shyness in an adult should be severely penalized.

Disqualifications

1. Any deviation from the height prescribed in the Standard.
2. A thoroughly pink nose or one lacking in any pigment.
3. Eye rims without pigment.
4. Docking or otherwise altering the length or natural carriage of the tail.
5. Any other color or combination of colors other than black, yellow or chocolate as described in the Standard.

Approved February 12, 1994
Effective March 31, 1994

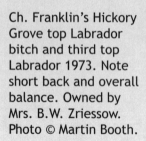

Ch. Franklin's Hickory Grove top Labrador bitch and third top Labrador 1973. Note short back and overall balance. Owned by Mrs. B.W. Zriessow. Photo © Martin Booth.

Am. Can. Ch. Sunnybrook Acres Ace O'Spade, U.D.T.X., W.C., the all-time top winning Labrador Retriever. owned by Dr. and Mrs. John H. Ippensen. Photo © Noel E. Johnson.

must travel at good speed if he is to be of value to the hunter. An extremely short-coupled Labrador Retriever would not be able to do this smoothly, because his rear legs would certainly outreach his body length and he would be forced to "sidewind" or "straddle-gait" in order to avoid stepping on his own front feet. The balance of the length of back is extremely important in moving. A dog that is properly balanced moves smoothly and comfortably and is a willing and active worker.

The head is to have a moderate stop. Dogs with heavy English breeding appear to have a more pronounced stop and a somewhat larger head. This difference is obvious from ringside. Equal length of skull and muzzle gives a nicely balanced proportion to the head. Brown or hazel are the preferred eye colors, while black or yellow eyes are undesirable. Admittedly, this may be an aesthetic evaluation, but it is one that is of concern to many breeders.

The neck seems to be one of the problem areas in the breed today. There currently are

A head study of
FC and AFC Car-
Lab Penrod,
owned by August
and Louise
Belmont.

many short-necked specimens in the ring. The problem seems to be a combination of a less-than-medium-length neck plus straight shoulders, which only exaggerates the situation, making the neck appear shorter than it really is. Dogs with this problem usually also have a very thick neck and appear to be throaty.

Good width and depth of chest must be in proportion to the overall substance of the dog. A small dog or bitch that carries less bone will be a smaller-chested specimen, but a number of barrel-chested examples also can be seen today.

The hindquarters are to be well muscled and powerful. This is most important in a breed that was developed for the field. A weak-reared dog would not have the drive and sustaining power to move out across the field and to leap into the water to retrieve fowl. The leaping ability is determined by the rear musculature. A good bend of stifle allows the dog to get under himself and supplies the driving action. Straight-stifled dogs have a stiff-legged,

up-and-down motion and have very little drive.

A dog that does not have straight front legs usually has poorly formed shoulders. Many times, this is the result of poor proportion between the scapula and the humerus. If one of these bones is too short, the dog will have a tendency to toe-out so that he can maintain his standing balance. The momentum of movement may make the problem less noticeable, but it will still exist.

Long legs can make a dog appear short coupled, when in reality he is not. It is again a question of proportion and balance. Most long-legged dogs appear to be short backed. They are, however, unbalanced, and upon careful analysis are discovered to be top heavy. A leggy dog would be an inefficient retriever, because he would not be as good a swimmer as a dog with medium-length legs.

The tail is truly a distinctive feature of the Labrador Retriever. The thick, round, almost furlike tail is an easily recognizable characteristic of the breed. Sparsely coated tails are more like those of pointers. Some breeders whose dogs' tails are rather heavily feathered trim them to make them round and otterlike. This, of course, does not eliminate the problem, because it will be reproduced in succeeding generations.

The coat of the Labrador Retriever must be dense and hard or even coarse to the touch if he is to be a good field dog. Having been bred as a water dog for a very cold climate, the Labrador must have a double coat that is correct for that purpose. The density of the soft undercoat will protect the dog from the elements, while the hardness of the outercoat will prevent the coat from absorbing water while he is swimming. A specimen with an overly soft or cottony coat would absorb water too easily and weigh the dog down in the water.

Coat color is more a matter of personal preference than anything else as long as the quality of the color is good. While a small spot of white on the chest is permissible in all three colors, it is not desirable. In both the yellows and the chocolates, subtle variations of the basic color occur. With the lighter-colored dogs, provision is also made for the lightening of the nose color in winter. This is merely a seasonal situation and is self-correcting. While brown- and liver-colored noses are acceptable on the lighter-colored dogs, many breeders still prefer the very dark brown or black noses. The Dudley, or pink, nose that is permanently without pigment is now a disqualification.

Movement is hard to describe on paper but is easily understood when watching a Labrador Retriever move across an open field. Many Breed Standards refer to "free and effortless movement," which, in reality, is merely an indication that the bone and muscle balance of the dog is correct. This, of course, results in a dog that can do the work for which he was bred for a considerable period of time without tiring. This is an important quality for a field dog.

The Labrador Retriever should not move as frantically as a coursing hound, nor as determinedly as a scent hound. He was bred to move out efficiently as a retriever and to return promptly with the bird. While speed is a good quality for the breed, it is not to be rated above the *trueness* of his movement. Wasted motion caused by paddling or sidewinding would be very tiring and would make for an inefficient worker. The movement, both coming and going, should be clean and precise, without feet, elbows, or hocks breaking the symmetry of the gait.

Standards for height and weight are easily understood, but because there was no disqualification prior to 1994, they were ignored by many breeders and judges who felt that they served only as a guide rather than as a rigid limit. As a result, the breed has been growing somewhat smaller with the passing years. Size differences even appear in various parts of the country. Because of the difficulty and the cost of shipping a bitch to be bred, many breeders used only local studs. This is a concern in all of the large breeds of dogs. Very small dogs are more readily shipped for breeding and as a result appear more standardized than some of the larger breeds. As more and more regulations are put on the air shipment of dogs, this problem will become even more noticeable.

With the revision of the Standard in 1994, undersized and oversized dogs are now disqualified. The size requirements are what they have always been, but dogs that do not fall within these limits are now disqualified.

The Labrador Retriever is a moderate dog both in overall size and in balance. The adjectives "moderate" and "medium" are used throughout the Standard. This emphasis is a clear statement that neither the large specimens nor the small specimens will serve the function for which the breed was created, which is to be a tireless, working field dog.

Multiple Best in Show winning Ch. Timmberland Golden Star, owned by Jan Stolarevsky of Ambersand Labradors. Photo by Martin Booth photography.

SELECTING A LABRADOR RETRIEVER PUPPY

When you have decided that a Labrador Retriever will be the ideal dog for your family, you still need to make several other decisions before undertaking the final selection of a puppy. You need to determine if the dog will just be the family companion and mascot, or whether he will be used for retrieving during the hunting season or for field trials and hunting tests. There is also the option of a bench-type dog for conformation classes at the shows sponsored by the American Kennel Club. The prices for these various types of dogs differ greatly. Pet-quality dogs range in price from $100 to $300, while dogs for the showring will usually range from about $500 and up. Started hunting dogs will range from $400 to $1,000, while fully trained and proven working retrievers can cost several thousand dollars.

With the Labrador Retriever, there is also the option of color choice—the blacks, the yellows, and the chocolates. One color is of no greater significance than another, so the choice is merely a matter of personal taste.

How does one pick from such an adorable litter? These pups were bred by Erik Bergishagen, Jagersbo Labradors.

Whenever possible, ask to see the parents of the puppies.
Photo © Kent and Donna Dannen.

Because the purchase of a family dog is not an everyday occurrence, you should do a certain amount of planning before actually buying a puppy. You are well advised to make several trips to well-established Labrador Retriever breeding kennels, attend at least one dog show, and attend a field trial or hunting test to see examples of the breed at various stages of development, from puppy to full-grown adult.

Once you have taken the preliminary steps, and your family decides to buy a Labrador Retriever, then select a reputable kennel for your purchase. If there is a local kennel club and it has a breeder-referral service, the problem is simplified. However, because so many towns do not have such a service available, it might be necessary to consult the American Kennel Club, which does offer a breeder-referral service through the parent breed clubs. There are also national dog magazines that usually contain classified advertisements arranged in a geographical index. This will simplify finding a kennel within driving distance. Located

across the country are a number of breeders who are dedicated to the betterment of the breed and who will make a great effort in helping you find just the right puppy. In larger cities, the classified section of the newspaper will have a column advertising pets for sale. This is also a valuable source of information for finding a kennel.

If you want a Labrador Retriever that you can train for the field, purchase him only from a reputable kennel. Sires and dams that have earned AKC championships and have been given the title of Field Champion (FC), Amateur Field Champion (AFC), Junior Hunter (JH), Senior Hunter (SH) , Master Hunter (MH), CD, CDX, or titles presented by other legitimate retriever organizations, are more likely to produce successful retrieving progeny than are dogs of questionable lineage. Ask for a copy of the puppy's pedigree and carefully study the last three generations. Most good breeders will gladly provide you with any information you want.

A puppy should not be taken from his mother before he is eight weeks old. He may be weaned by the time he is six weeks of age, but the extra two weeks will give him greater stamina and more confidence when he finally does leave home. The puppy also has additional time to adjust to a solid-food diet, and the breeder has time to have the puppy checked for worms and other parasites and to have him inoculated.

Photo © Kent and Donna Dannen.

Decide ahead of time if you want a chocolate, black, or yellow Lab, or if the color really doesn't matter to you. Photos © Kent and Donna Dannen.

When there are several puppies from which to choose, you have an opportunity to see the personality of each puppy as he relates to the rest of the litter. Whether you are intrigued by the most aggressive and outgoing puppy, or you develop a protective attitude toward the most shy and retiring individual, you do get a clue to the future personality of the dog by observing this puppy play. Maturity and a new home environment can certainly modify a personality, but usually some of the original traits will remain.

While watching the puppy romp, you will be able to verify that he does not limp or does not have any other obvious physical disability. Examine the puppy to ascertain that his eyes are clear and that he has no sores or cuts on his body. Once this superficial examination has been completed, you have an opportunity to make other rather subjective decisions, such as those relating to size and overall balance. In many cases, however, you may fall in love with a particular puppy and will decide to buy that one regardless of other factors. Dogs are frequently sold to compulsive buyers, but this is not the best way to make your decision!

If you are choosing a puppy to train for the field, about the only thing you can do beyond studying the puppy's pedigree is to select an individual that has good conformation, one that is about the average size for the litter, one that has no obvious defects (such as an overbite), one that seems to be aggressive, and finally, one that you would just plain like to have because he appeals to you. You also must decide whether to choose a male or female. This choice is strictly a matter of personal preference. The male is by nature the more aggressive, but your training methods will be the same regardless of the sex of the dog.

FIRST DAYS
IN THE NEW HOME

As soon as the puppy arrives at his new home, allow him to romp in a fenced exercise area in the yard. This will establish, from the first moment he is in his new home, that

Give your puppy some toys to chew on. Puppies cut teeth off and on for the first seven months or so. Photo © Robert and Eunice Pearcy.

he must do certain things outside. Returning him to this same place on a fixed schedule will start the housebreaking pattern promptly and should prove to be a most effective method.

Within a day or two after your purchase, take the puppy to the veterinarian. The puppy undoubtedly will have been given a temporary shot by the kennel owner from whom he was purchased, but this temporary shot will be good for only about two weeks. A permanent inoculation can be given when the puppy is three

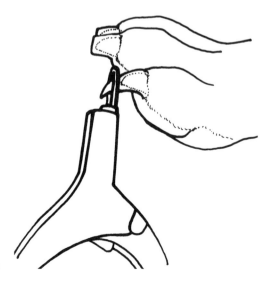

Trimming the nail.

months old. This precaution is extremely important for your puppy's health.

There are several common diseases to which dogs are susceptible, such as distemper, hepatitis, leptospirosis and parvo virus. These diseases are serious because they are frequently fatal when immunization has been neglected. Even though they are serious diseases, there are effective inoculations against them and several other diseases. Your veterinarian will recommend a safe vaccination protocol and schedule. You also need to inoculate your dog against rabies at an age specified by local laws. Again, follow your veterinarian's recommendation.

While the puppy is at your veterinarian's office, he should have his nails clipped. Long nails cause discomfort when he walks. Learn to clip your dog's nails, because they must be clipped every week or two. Learning to perform this simple chore can save you a great deal of money over a period of time. Also while at the veterinarian's office, have your puppy's ears examined to see that they are free from wax. Have him examined for worms and other parasites.

A competent veterinarian will keep a Labrador Retriever in good health and assure a life of ten to fifteen years, as well as keep you free from needless care and worry. Selecting the right veterinarian warrants serious consideration.

REGISTERING YOUR PUPPY

When you purchase a puppy, you will receive from the breeder a registration application issued by the AKC and a copy of the dog's pedigree. The registration application will contain the information required to complete the transfer of ownership from the breeder to you. The paper contains information such as the name of the sire and the dam, the date of birth, the color and sex of the puppy, and the registration number of the litter.

At the time of purchase, the breeder must provide certain information on the

Socialize your puppy to different outdoor and indoor environments. Photo © Kent and Donna Dannen.

reverse side of the registration application. This will transfer the registration of ownership to you. The application must be signed both by the seller and by you and forwarded to the AKC along with the necessary fee as specified on the application.

When filling in the information on the front side of the application, you also will have an opportunity to name the puppy. Sometimes the breeder requests that the kennel prefix be included in the name of the dog. This allows the breeder to keep track of his dogs if they are entered in AKC shows, field trials, or hunting tests.

The AKC has established a limited or restricted registration policy for dogs. This puts a limitation on the future use of the dog. The breeder, at the time of sale, determines whether or not the dog should ever be used for breeding either because of genetic problems or simply to keep down overpopulation of the breed. This limited-registration certificate ensures that any offspring of this dog can never be registered.

When the certificate is returned by the AKC, keep it a safe place, because it represents the title of ownership of the dog. Information contained in this document

A well-socialized puppy learns to accept strangers. Take him to places such as a shopping mall, park, or training center. Photo © Click the Photo Connection.

Puppies are full
of surprises.
Photo © Robert
and Eunice
Pearcy.

will be needed if the dog is ever entered in competition at a sanctioned show, trial, or test or if the dog is used for breeding.

The AKC offers additional services for the owner. Its Home Again registration service is available to dogs that have been tattooed or microchipped for identifica-

tion. If the dog is lost, a call to the hotline can identify the owner and facilitate relocation. Another service is a certified pedigree of the dog, which contains much useful information for the breeder, show or field trial owner.

RAISING THE LABRADOR RETRIEVER

EQUIPMENT

It is much easier to adapt to the demands of a new Labrador Retriever puppy if you collect the necessary equipment before bringing your puppy home. The two basic items are a water dish and a food dish. These should be of stainless steel so that they cannot be chewed, and they should have flared sides to prevent their being tipped over. Other items will include chew toys, a soft puppy leash, and a pin-hair brush for grooming. You will need to select a place for the puppy's bed and prepare his bedding material.

Every dog should have a bed of his own, snug and warm, where he can retire undisturbed when he wishes to nap. This is especially true with the young puppy. It is desirable to have the bed arranged so that the dog can be securely confined at times, safe and contented. If the puppy is taught early in life to stay quietly in his box at night, or when the family is out, the habit will carry over into adulthood and will benefit both dog and master.

BEDDING AND CRATES

Never banish your dog to a damp, cold basement. Keep him quartered in an out-of-the-way corner close to the center of

Canadian Ch. Pine Edge Shifftin' Gears, J.H., C.D., A.W.C., C.W.C., owned by Nancy Brandow. Photo © Chuck and Sandy Tatham.

29

family activity. His bed can be an elaborate, cushioned affair with an electric warming pad or simply a rectangular wooden box or heavy cardboard carton, cushioned with a clean cotton rug or towel. Actually, the latter is ideal for a new puppy, because it is snug, easy to clean, and expendable. A door can be cut in one side of the box for easy access, but it should be placed in such a way that the dog can still be confined when desirable.

The crates used by breeders and professional handlers at dog shows and trials make ideal indoor quarters. They are lightweight but strong, provide adequate air circulation, yet are snug and warm and easily cleaned. If you take your dog along when you travel, a dog crate is ideal. Your dog will willingly stay in his accustomed bed during long automobile trips, and the crate can be taken into motels or hotels at night, making the dog a far more acceptable guest.

Dog crates are made of chromed metal, plastic, or wood, and some have tops covered with a special rubber matting so that they can be used as grooming tables. Anyone modestly handy with tools can construct such a crate.

Crates come in different sizes to suit various breeds of dogs. For reasons of economy, the size selected for the Labrador Retriever puppy should be adequate for use when the dog is full grown. The standard Labrador crate measures thirty-six inches by twenty-six inches by twenty-four inches. If the area seems too large when the puppy is small, a temporary cardboard partition can be installed to limit the area he occupies. For your convenience, and to enhance your dog's sense of security, keep food and water dishes in the same general area where you keep the crate.

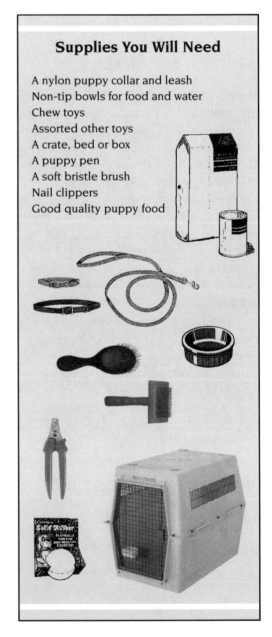

Supplies You Will Need

A nylon puppy collar and leash
Non-tip bowls for food and water
Chew toys
Assorted other toys
A crate, bed or box
A puppy pen
A soft bristle brush
Nail clippers
Good quality puppy food

Every dog needs his own bed, whether it is a luxurious store model, a crate, or a cardboard box. Photo © Click the Photo Connection.

NUTRITION

The main food elements required by Labrador Retrievers are proteins, fats, and carbohydrates. Vitamins A, B complex, D, and E are essential, as are ample amounts of calcium and iron. Nine other minerals are required in small amounts but are amply provided in almost any diet, so there is little need to be concerned about them.

The most important nutrient is protein, and it must be provided every day of your dog's life. Protein is essential for normal daily growth and replacement of body tissues burned up in daily activity. Preferred animal protein products are beef, mutton, horse meat, and boned fish. Visceral organs—heart, liver, and tripe—are good, but if they are given in quantities that are too large, they may cause diarrhea. Bone marrow in large amounts can have the same effect. Some veterinarians feel that pork is undesirable, while others consider lean pork acceptable as long as it is well cooked. Bacon drippings are often recommended for inclusion in the dog's diet, but this is a matter best discussed with your veterinarian, because the salt in the bacon drippings might prove harmful to a dog that is not in good health. The meat meal used in some commercial foods is made from scrap meat processed at high temperatures and then dried. It is not as nutritious as fresh meat, but when it is combined with other protein products, it is an acceptable ingredient in your dog's diet.

Cooked eggs and raw egg yolks are good sources of protein, but never feed your dog raw egg white because it may cause diarrhea. Cottage cheese and milk, either fresh, dried, or canned, are high in protein. Puppies thrive on milk, and it is usually included in the diet until the puppy is about three months of age. When fed to older dogs, however, it often causes diarrhea. Soybean meal, wheat-germ meal, and dried brewer's yeast are vegetable products high in protein and may be used to advantage in your dog's diet.

Use vegetable and animal fats in moderate amounts, especially if a main ingredient of your dog's diet is dry or kibbled food. Never use fats excessively or your dog may become overweight. Generally, increase fats slightly in the winter and reduce them somewhat during warm weather.

Carbohydrates are required for proper assimilation of fats. Dog biscuits, kibble, dog meal, and other dehydrated foods are good sources of carbohydrates, as are cereal products derived from rice, corn, wheat, and oats.

Vegetables supply additional proteins, vitamins, and minerals, and by providing bulk are of value in overcoming constipation. Raw or cooked carrots, celery, lettuce, beets, asparagus, tomatoes, and cooked spinach may be used. They should always be chopped or ground well and mixed with the other food. Various combinations may be used, but a good home-mixed ration for the mature dog consists of two parts of meat and one each of vegetables and dog meal or cereal products.

Dicalcium phosphate and cod-liver oil are added to puppy diets to ensure inclusion of adequate amounts of calcium and vitamins A and D. Indiscriminate use of dietary supplements is not only unjustified but

Boiled shank bones or commercially available dog chews will help keep your puppy's teeth clean and his gums healthy. Photo © Robert and Eunice Pearcy.

Keep a non-tip bowl of fresh water available at all times.
Photo © Click the Photo Connection.

may be harmful, and many breeders feel that their overuse may lead to excessive growth as well as to overweight at maturity. Also, kidney damage in adult dogs has been traced to oversupplementation of the diet with calcium and vitamin D.

Foods manufactured by well-known and reputable food processors are nutritionally sound and are offered in a sufficient variety of flavors, textures, and consistencies that most dogs will find them tempting and satisfying. Canned foods are usually ready to eat, while dehydrated foods in the form of kibble, meal, or biscuits may require the addition of water or milk. Dried foods containing fat sometimes become rancid, and to avoid an unpalatable change in flavor, the manufacturer may not include fat in dried food but recommend its addition at the time the water or milk is added.

Candy and other sweets are taboo, because the dog has no nutritional need for them and if he is permitted to eat them, he will usually eat less of the food he requires. Also taboo are fried foods, highly seasoned foods, and extremely starchy foods, because the dog's digestive tract is not equipped to handle them.

Thaw frozen foods completely and warm them at least to a lukewarm temperature. Cool hot foods to lukewarm. Food should be in a fairly firm state, because sloppy food is difficult for the dog to digest.

Whether meat is raw or cooked makes little difference, as long as you give your dog the juice that seeps from the meat during cooking. Bones provide little nourishment, although gnawing bones helps make the teeth strong and helps to keep tartar from accumulating on them. Beef bones, especially four- to five-inch sections of shank bone, are best. These bones can be boiled to remove the marrow and the grease so that they will not stain the carpet when your Labrador Retriever drags one into the living room to chew on. The flavor remains in the bone, but not the grease, and shank bones do not splinter when chewed. Never give fish, poultry, and chop bones to your dog because they tend to splinter and may puncture your dog's digestive tract.

Clean, fresh, cool water is essential. Be sure that your puppy has an adequate supply twenty-four hours a day from the time he is big enough to walk. Especially during hot weather, the drinking pan should be emptied and refilled at frequent intervals.

Puppies usually are weaned by the time they are six weeks old. When you acquire a puppy that is ten or twelve weeks old, he already will have been started on a feeding schedule. The breeder should supply exact details regarding the number of meals a day, the types and amounts of food offered, and the names and types of any other regular dietary supplements. It is essential to adhere to this established routine, for drastic changes in diet may produce intestinal upsets. Two meals a day are recommended. In most instances, a combination of dry meal, canned meat, and the plastic-wrapped hamburger-like products provide a well-balanced diet. For a puppy that is too fat or too thin, or for one that has health problems, a veterinarian may recommend a specially formulated diet, but ordinarily the commercially prepared foods can be used. A puppy is considered to be in correct weight when his ribs do not show but rather feel covered with firm flesh.

The amount of food offered at each meal must gradually be increased, and by five months of age, the puppy will require about twice the amount he needed when he was three months of age. However, do not allow your puppy to become too fat. Obesity has become a major health problem for dogs, and it is estimated that 40 percent of American dogs are overweight. It is essential that weight be controlled throughout your dog's lifetime and that your dog be kept in trim condition—neither too fat nor too thin—because many physical problems can be traced directly to overweight. If the habit of overeating is developed in puppyhood, it will be much more difficult to control the weight of your mature dog.

A mature dog usually eats slightly less than he did as a growing puppy. For dogs more than one year old, one large meal a day is usually sufficient, although you may prefer to give two meals. As long as your dog enjoys optimum health and is neither too fat nor too thin, the number of meals per day makes little difference.

The amount of food required for a mature Labrador Retriever will vary. The adult male weighs between sixty-five and eighty pounds and the bitch between fifty-five and seventy pounds. With canned dog food or home-prepared foods that are a combination of meat, vegetables, and meal, the approximate amount required is one-half ounce of food per pound of body weight. If the dog is fed a commercial dry food, approximately one ounce of food is needed for each pound of body weight. Most manufacturers of commercial foods provide information on the packages as to approximate daily needs of various breeds. For most dogs, the amount of food should be increased slightly during the winter months and reduced somewhat during hot weather when the dog is less active.

As a dog becomes older and less active, he may become too fat, or his appetite may decrease and he may become too thin. It is necessary to adjust the diet in either case, because your dog will live longer and enjoy better health if he is maintained in trim condition. The simplest way to decrease or increase body weight is by decreasing or increasing the amount of fat in the diet. Maintain the protein content at a high level throughout your dog's life.

If the older Labrador Retriever becomes reluctant to eat, it may be necessary to coax him with the special food he normally relishes. Warming the food will increase its aroma and usually will help to entice the dog to eat. If he still refuses, rubbing some of the food on the

Two more require-ments for a healthy, happy Labrador: plenty of love and atten-tion, and his own toys, particularly those made for retrieving. Photo © Karen Hudson.

dog's lips and gums may stimulate inter-est. It may be helpful also to offer food in smaller amounts and increase the number of meals per day. Foods that are highly nu-tritious and easily digested are especially desirable for older dogs. Small amounts of cooked ground liver, cottage cheese, or mashed, hard-cooked eggs should fre-quently be included in the diet.

Before a bitch is bred, make sure that she is in optimum condition, slightly on the lean side rather than the fat side. The bitch in whelp is given much the same diet she was fed prior to breeding, with slight increases in amounts of meat, liver, and dairy products. Beginning about six weeks after breeding, she should be fed two meals per day rather than one, and the total daily intake should be increased. Some bitches in whelp require as much as 50 percent more food than they con-sumed before breeding. Do not permit your bitch to become fat, because whelp-ing problems are more likely to occur in overweight dogs. Cod-liver oil and dical-cium phosphate should be provided until the puppies are weaned.

The stud dog used only occasionally for breeding will not require a special diet, but he should be well fed and maintained in optimum condition. A dog used fre-quently at stud may require a slightly in-creased amount of food, but his basic diet will require no change as long as his gen-eral health is good and his flesh is firm and hard.

MANNERS FOR YOUR LABRADOR RETRIEVER

Although each Labrador Retriever has personality traits and idiosyncrasies that set him apart as an individual, dogs in general have two characteristics that can be utilized to advantage in training. The first is the dog's strong desire to please, which has been built up through centuries of association with people. The second lies in the innate quality of the dog's mentality. It has been proven conclusively that while dogs have reasoning power, their learning ability is based on a direct association of cause and effect, so that they willingly repeat acts that bring pleasant results and discontinue acts that bring unpleasant results. Hence, to take fullest advantage of your dog's abilities, you must make sure that your dog understands a command, then reward him when he obeys and correct him when he does not.

Make commands as short as possible and repeat them in the same way, day after day. Saying "Heel" one day and "Come here and heel" the next day will confuse your dog. *Heel, sit, stand, stay, down,* and *come* are standard terminology and are preferable for a dog that may later be given advanced training.

Tone of voice is important, too. For instance, a coaxing tone helps cajole a young puppy into trying something new. Once an exercise is mastered, commands given in a firm, matter-of-fact voice give the dog confidence in his own ability. Praise, expressed in an exuberant tone, will tell your dog quite clearly that he has earned your approval. On the other hand, a firm "No" indicates with equal clarity that he has done something wrong.

Rewards for a good performance may consist simply of praising lavishly and petting your dog, although many professional trainers use bits of food as rewards. Tidbits are effective only if the dog is hungry, of course. If you smoke, be sure to wash your hands before each training session, because the odor of nicotine is repulsive to dogs. On the hands of a heavy smoker, the odor of nicotine may be so strong that the dog is unable to smell a tidbit.

Correction for wrongdoing should be limited to repeating "No" in a scolding tone of voice or to confining the dog to his bed or crate. Spanking or striking the dog is taboo. This is particularly true in using sticks for punishment, because they may cause injury. Slapping your dog with your hand is no better of a solution. Dogs that have been punished by slapping have a tendency to cringe whenever they see a hand raised and consequently do not respond promptly when your intent is not to punish but to signal.

Some trainers recommend correcting a dog by whacking him with a rolled-up

Reneway Maudie of Ashridge, C.D., J.H., owned by C. Baugh, has learned to lie quietly on a grooming table. Photo by C.H. Brown.

newspaper. The idea is that the newspaper will not injure the dog, but the resulting noise will condition the dog to avoid repeating the act that seemingly caused the noise. Many authorities object to this type of correction, because it may result in the dog becoming noise shy. This is a decided disadvantage with show dogs that must maintain poise in adverse, often noisy, situations. Noise shyness is also an unfortunate reaction in field dogs, because it may lead to gunshyness—an unacceptable situation for a hunting Labrador Retriever.

To be effective, correction must be administered immediately so that in the dog's mind there is a direct connection between his act and the correction. You can make voice corrections under almost any circumstances, but never call your dog to come and then give a correction, because your dog will associate the correction with the fact that he has come when called. Consequently, he will be reluctant to respond the next time. If the dog is at a distance and doing something he should not be doing, go to him and scold him while he is still involved in the wrongdoing. If this is impossible, ignore the error until he repeats it, then correct him properly.

Watch your Labrador Retriever closely and stop him before he gets into mischief, especially when he is young. All dogs need to do a certain amount of chewing. To prevent your puppy from chewing something of value, provide him with his own balls and toys. Never allow him to chew on castoff slippers, because he will have no way of knowing the difference between castoff items and other items that do have value. Nylon stockings, wooden articles, and similar objects may cause intestinal obstruction if the dog chews and swallows them. It is essential that you permit your dog to chew only on rawhide or on toys that he cannot chew up or swallow.

Serious obedience training for the Labrador Retriever should not be started until the dog has had all of the basic training necessary for good citizenship. Basic training in house manners should begin, however, the day your puppy enters his new home. Never give your puppy the run of the house. Confine him to a box or a small pen except for play periods when he can have your full attention.

The first thing to teach your dog is his name, so that whenever he hears it, he will immediately come to attention. Whenever you are near the box, talk to your puppy and say his name repeatedly. During play periods, talk to your dog, pet him, and handle him. It is important that he be conditioned so that he will not object to being handled by a family friend, a veterinarian, or even a show judge at a later date. As your dog investigates his surroundings, watch him carefully, and if he tries to do something that he should not do, reprimand him with a scolding "No!" If he repeats the offense, scold him and confine him to his box. Discipline must be prompt, consistent, and always followed with praise. Never tease your dog, and never allow others to do so. Kindness and understanding are essential to a pleasant, mutually rewarding relationship.

When the puppy is two to three months old, it is time to purchase a flat, narrow leather collar and have the dog start wearing it at all times. Never use a harness, because this will only encourage your dog to tug and to pull. After a week or so, attach a light leather leash to the collar during play sessions and let your puppy walk around, dragging the leash behind him. Then start holding the end of the leash and coaxing your puppy to come when called. He will then be fully accustomed to the collar and the leash when it is time to train him for companion walking.

HOUSE TRAINING

Housebreaking can be accomplished in a matter of approximately two weeks, provided the dog is mature enough to have some control over bodily functions. This is usually about three months of age, but many Labrador Retrievers respond to such training several weeks earlier. Until that time, the puppy should spend most of his day confined to his penned area, with the floor covered with several layers of newspapers so that he may relieve himself when necessary without damage to the floor.

Either of two methods works well in housebreaking, with the choice depending on the housing arrangements. In a house with a readily accessible yard, it is wise to start training your puppy outdoors from the very beginning. If the dog lives with you in an apartment without easy access to a fenced yard, it may be necessary to paper train the dog at first and then, when he has learned control, to teach him to relieve himself outdoors.

If you do not want your Labrador to get on the furniture, start teaching him the word "No!" while he is young. Photo © Robert and Eunice Pearcy.

If you decide to train your puppy by taking him outdoors, confine him while he is indoors so he can be watched. One of the small commercial puppy pens makes an excellent training ground. Dogs are naturally clean animals, reluctant to soil their living quarters, and confining your puppy to a limited area will encourage him to avoid making a mess.

A young puppy must be taken out often. Watch him carefully so that when he gives any indication that he is about to relieve himself, you can take him out at once. If he has an accident, scold him and take him out immediately so that he will associate the act of going outside with the need to relieve himself. Always take your puppy out after eating. Take him to the same place to relieve himself so that he will associate this spot with that activity. Restrict your puppy's access to water about two hours before you put him to bed. Take him out the last thing before retiring, and then again the first thing in the morning before he is fully awake and has an opportunity to relieve himself in the house.

For paper training, set aside a particular area and cover it with several layers of

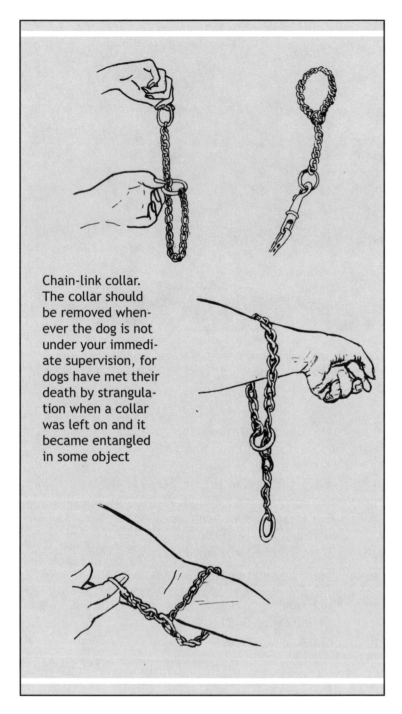

Chain-link collar. The collar should be removed whenever the dog is not under your immediate supervision, for dogs have met their death by strangulation when a collar was left on and it became entangled in some object

himself. As he comes to understand the idea, the paper-covered area can be decreased until it is only the size of a double page of newspaper. Keep your dog using the papers, but begin taking him out on a leash at the same time every day in order to structure his habits. Also, at the first sign that he needs to relieve himself, take him outdoors.

Using either method, the Labrador Retriever puppy will be housebroken in an amazingly short time. Once he has learned control, he will need to relieve himself only four or five times a day.

OBEDIENCE TRAINING

Informal obedience training, started when the puppy is three or four months old, will provide a good background for any advanced training that the dog might receive at a later date. The collar most effective for training is the metal chain-link variety. The correct size for the dog will be about one inch longer than the measurement around the largest part of the dog's head. Slip the chain through one of the rings so that the collar forms a loop. Put the collar on with the loose ring to the right of the dog's neck. The chain or leash attached to the collar should come over the neck and through the holding ring, rather than under the neck. Because the dog is to be at your left side for most of the training, this makes the collar most effective.

Attach the leash to the loose ring. The leash should be either webbing or leather, six feet long, and at least a half inch wide. To get your dog's attention, or to give him a correction, it is only necessary to give a light, quick pull on the leash, which will momentarily tighten the collar around the neck. Release the pressure immediately. If your puppy is already accustomed to a leather collar, he will adjust easily to the training collar. It is necessary to have your dog fully trained to walk on a leash before you start any formal obedience training. This will prepare him for the use of the collar as a correcting tool.

newspapers. Confine the dog to this area, and each time he relieves himself, remove the soiled papers and replace them with clean ones.

As your Labrador Retriever's ability to control himself increases, gradually decrease the size of the paper-covered area. If he uses the bare floor, scold him mildly and put him on the paper, letting him know that *there* is where he is to relieve

Six-foot leash.

A puppy picture of American and Canadian Ch. Ashridge Clementine, owned by C. Baugh.

It is ideal to set aside a period of about fifteen minutes, once or twice a day, for regular training sessions, and to train in a place where there will be no distractions. Teach only one exercise at a time, making sure that your dog has mastered it before going on to another. It will probably take at least a week for your Labrador Retriever to master each exercise. As training progresses, start each session by reviewing exercises your dog has already mastered before going on to the new exercise. When discipline is required, make the correction immediately, and always praise your dog after a correction as well as when he obeys promptly. During each session, stick strictly to business. Afterwards, take time to play with your dog.

The first exercise to teach is heeling. Have your dog on your left side and hold the leash in your right hand. Start walking, and just before taking the first step, say your dog's name to get his attention and then give the command "Heel!" Simultaneously, pull lightly on the leash. Keep your dog on your left side, with his head alongside your left leg. Pull on your dog's leash as necessary to urge him forward or backward, to the right or to the left, but keep him in position. Each time the leash is pulled, give the command "Heel!" then praise your dog lavishly. When your dog heels properly in a straight line, it is time to start making circles, turning corners, and introducing the other exercises that will be required in an obedience or field trial.

Once your dog has learned to heel well, it is time to start teaching the command "Sit." Each time you stop while heeling, give the command "Sit." The dog will be on your left side so that you can use your left hand to press down on your dog's hindquarters and guide him into a sitting position. The leash, still held in your right hand, can keep your dog's head up. Hold this position for a few moments while you praise your dog. Then give the command to heel again. After taking a few steps, stop your dog and repeat the procedure. While

A Labrador and his owner perform the "heel off lead" exercise in an obedience class. Photo © Judith Strom.

your dog is taught to sit on the left side, he can be taught to sit from any position.

When your dog will sit on command without correction, he is ready to learn to stay until he is released. Simply sit him, then give the command "Stay" and hold him in position for perhaps half a minute, repeating "Stay!" if he attempts to stand. Release him with "O.K." Gradually increase the time until he will stay on command for three or four minutes.

The stand-stay command should also be taught when your dog is on leash. While you are heeling your dog, stop and give the command "Stand!" Keep your dog from sitting by placing your left arm under him, immediately in front of his right rear leg. If he continues to try to sit, do not scold him, but start up again with the heel command, walk several steps, and stop again, repeating the stand command and preventing your dog from sitting. Once your dog has mastered the stand, teach him to stay by holding him in position and repeating the word "Stay!"

The down-stay will prove beneficial in many situations, but especially when you take your dog without confining him in a crate. To teach the down, have your dog sitting at your side with his collar and leash on. Step forward with the leash in your hand and turn to face your dog. Let the leash touch the floor, then step over it with your right foot so that it is under the instep of your shoe. Grasping the leash low with both hands, slowly pull up, saying "Down!" Hold the leash taut until your dog goes down. Once he responds well, teach your dog to stay in the down position with the down-stay command using the same method as for the sit-stay and the stand-stay commands.

The "come" command is taught when your dog is on leash and heeling. Simply walk along, then suddenly take a step backward, saying "Come!" Pull the leash while giving the command, and your dog will turn and follow. Continue walking backward, repeatedly saying "Come," and tightening the leash if necessary.

Once your dog has mastered the exercises while on leash, teach these same exercises off leash, going through the same routine by beginning with heeling. If your dog does not respond promptly, he needs to review these commands with the leash on. Patience and persistence will be rewarded, for you will have a dog that you can trust to respond promptly under all conditions.

CORRECTING BAD HABITS

Even after your Labrador Retriever is well trained, he sometimes develops bad habits that are hard to break. Jumping on people is a common habit, and all members of the family must assist if it is to be broken. Because the Labrador Retriever is a large dog, take a step forward and raise your knee just as your dog starts to jump up. As your knee strikes the dog's chest, give the command "Down!" in a scolding voice. With this method, your dog is taken by surprise and does not associate the discomfort with the person causing it.

Occasionally a dog may be too friendly with guests who do not care for dogs. If your dog has had obedience training, he

Ch. Cedarwood's Master Band, J.H., C.D., W.C.I., T.D.I., owned by Carl and Nancy Brandow.

can be commanded to sit or down beside you.

Persistent efforts may be needed to subdue a dog that barks without provocation. To correct this habit, you must be close to your dog when he starts barking. Encircle his muzzle with both hands, hold his mouth shut, and command "Quiet!" in a firm voice. He should soon learn to respond so that he can be controlled by simply giving him the command.

Sniffing other dogs is an annoying habit. If your dog is off leash and sniffs other dogs, ignoring commands to come, he needs to review the lessons on basic be-

havior. When your dog is on leash, scold him, then pull on the leash, command "Heel," and walk away from the other dog.

A well-trained Labrador Retriever will be no problem if you decide that he will accompany you on trips. No matter how well he responds, however, he should never be permitted off leash when he is being walked in a strange area. Distractions will be more tempting, and there will be more of a chance of his being attacked by other dogs. The best advice for traveling with a dog is to take along his collar and leash, then use them.

Ch. Agber Daise of Cambellcroft, C.D., W.C., and Ch. Amaretto of Campbellcroft, C.D.X., J.H., W.C., owned by Donald and Virginia Campbell.

CANINE HEALTH CONDITIONS

Simple measures of preventive care are always preferable to cures that may be complicated and costly. Many of the problems that afflict dogs can be avoided easily by instituting good practices and procedures with your dog's feeding and housing.

Proper nutrition is essential in maintaining your dog's resistance to infectious disease, in reducing susceptibility to organic disease, and, of course, in preventing dietary deficiency diseases. Cleanliness is essential in preventing the growth of disease-producing bacteria and other microorganisms. All equipment, especially water and food dishes, must be kept immaculately clean. Cleanliness is also essential in controlling external parasites, which thrive in unsanitary surroundings.

SYMPTOMS OF ILLNESS

Symptoms of illness may be so obvious that there is no question that your dog is ill, or so subtle that you are not sure whether there is a change from normal or not. Loss of appetite, malaise (general lack of interest in what is going on), and vomiting may be ignored if they occur singly and persist only for a day. However, in combination with other evidence of illness, these symptoms may be significant, and you should watch your dog closely. Abnormal bowel movements, especially diarrhea or bloody stools, are causes for immediate concern. Urinary abnormalities may indicate infections, and bloody urine is always an indication of a serious condition. When a dog that has long been housebroken suddenly becomes incontinent, consult your veterinarian, for he may be able to suggest treatment or medication that will be helpful.

Fever is a positive indication of illness, and consistent deviation from the normal temperature range of 100°F to 102°F is cause for concern. Have your dog in a standing position when taking his temperature. Coat the bulb of a rectal thermometer with petroleum jelly, raise the dog's tail, insert the thermometer to approximately half its length, and hold it in position for two minutes. Clean the thermometer with rubbing alcohol after each use, and be sure to shake it down.

Fits, often considered a symptom of worms, may result from a variety of causes, including vitamin deficiencies, or playing to the point of exhaustion. Consult your veterinarian when a fit occurs, because it may be a symptom of serious illness.

Persistent coughing is often considered a symptom of worms but may also indicate heart trouble, especially in older dogs.

43

Ch. Breton Gate Cairngorm, C.D., W.C., owned by Donald and Virginia Campbell. Photo by Joan Ludwig.

Stary coat is a coat that is dull and lackluster and generally indicates poor health and possible worm infestation.

Dull eyes may result from similar conditions. Certain forms of blindness may also cause the eyes to lose the sparkle of vibrant good health.

Vomiting is another symptom often attributed to worm infestation. Dogs suffering from indigestion sometimes eat grass, apparently to induce vomiting and relieve discomfort.

ACCIDENTS AND INJURIES

Injuries of a serious nature such as deep cuts, broken bones, and severe burns always require veterinary care. However, your dog may need first aid before being moved to a veterinary hospital.

A dog injured in any way should be approached cautiously, because reactions of a dog in pain are unpredictable and he may even bite a beloved master. Always apply a muzzle before making any attempt to move your dog or treat him in any way. The muzzle can be improvised from a strip of cloth, a bandage, or even a heavy cord, looped firmly around the dog's jaw and tied under the lower jaw. Extend the ends to the back of the neck and tie them again so that the loop around the jaws will stay in place.

A stretcher for moving a heavy dog can be improvised from a rug or board, and preferably two people should be available to transport it. A small dog can be carried by one person simply by grasping the loose skin at the nape of the neck with one hand and placing the other hand under the dog's hips.

Burns from chemicals should first be treated by flushing the coat with plain water, taking care to protect the dog's eyes and ears. A baking-soda solution can then be applied to neutralize the chemical further. If the burned area is small, apply a bland ointment. If the burned area is large, more extensive treatment will be required, as well as veterinary care.

Burns from hot liquid or hot metals should be treated by applying a bland ointment, provided that the burned area is small. Burns over large areas should be treated by a veterinarian.

Electric shock usually results because you negligently left an electric cord exposed where your dog could chew on it. If possible, disconnect the cord before touching the dog. Otherwise, yank the cord from the dog's mouth so that you will not receive a shock when you try to help him. If your dog is unconscious, artificial respiration and stimulants will be required. Contact your veterinarian at once.

Fractures require immediate professional attention. A broken bone should be immobilized while the dog is transported to the veterinarian, but no attempt should be made to splint it.

Poisoning is more often accidental than deliberate, but whichever is the case, symptoms and treatment are the same. If the poisoning is not discovered immediately, the dog may be found unconscious. His mouth will be slimy, he will tremble, he will have difficulty breathing, and he may go into convulsions. Seek veterinary treatment immediately.

If you find your dog eating a poisonous substance, induce vomiting immediately by repeatedly forcing your dog to swallow a mixture of equal parts of hydrogen peroxide and water. Delay of even a few minutes may result in death. When the contents of the stomach have been emptied, force your dog to swallow raw egg white, which will slow the absorption of the poison. Then call your veterinarian. Provide him with information as to the type of poison, and follow his advice regarding additional treatment.

Some chemicals are toxic even if they are not swallowed. Before using a product, make sure that it can be used safely.

Severe bleeding from a leg can be controlled by applying a tourniquet between the wound and the body, but the tourniquet must be loosened at ten-minute intervals. Severe bleeding from the head or the body can be controlled by placing a cloth or gauze pad over the wound, then applying firm pressure with the hand.

To treat minor cuts, first trim the hair from around the wound, then wash the area with warm, soapy water and apply a mild antiseptic such as tincture of metaphen.

Shock is usually the aftermath of severe injury and requires immediate veterinary attention. The dog appears dazed, his lips and tongue are pale, and his breathing is shallow. Wrap your dog in blankets and keep him warm. If possible, keep him lying down with his head lower than his body.

BACTERIAL AND VIRAL DISEASES

Distemper takes many and varied forms, so it is sometimes difficult even for

Ch. Boradors Danny Boy, owned by Patricia A. Stark.

experienced veterinarians to diagnose it. It is the number-one killer of dogs, and although it is not unknown in older dogs, its victims are usually puppies. While some dogs do recover, permanent damage to the brain or nervous system is often sustained. Symptoms may include lethargy, diarrhea, vomiting, reduced appetite, cough, nasal discharge, inflammation of the eyes, and a rise in temperature. If distemper is suspected, a veterinarian must be consulted at once, for early treatment is essential. Effective preventive measures lie in inoculation. Shots for temporary immunity should be given to all puppies within a few weeks after whelping, and the permanent inoculations should be given as soon thereafter as possible.

Hardpad has been fairly prevalent in Great Britain for a number of years, and its incidence in the United States is increasing. Symptoms are similar to those of distemper, but as the disease progresses, the pads of the feet harden and eventually peel. Chances of recovery are not favorable unless prompt veterinary care is obtained.

Infectious hepatitis in dogs affects the liver, as does the human form, but apparently it is not transmissible to man. Symptoms are similar to those of distemper, and the disease rapidly reaches the acute state. Because hepatitis is often fatal, prompt veterinary treatment is essential. Effective vaccines are available and should be provided to all puppies. A combination distemper-hepatitis vaccine is sometimes used.

Leptospirosis is caused by a microorganism that is often transmitted by contact with rats or by ingestion of food contaminated by rats. The disease can be transmitted to man, and anyone caring for an afflicted dog must take steps to avoid infection. Symptoms include vomiting, loss of appetite, diarrhea, fever, depression and lethargy, redness of the eyes and gums, and sometimes jaundice. Permanent kidney damage may result, and veterinary treatment should be secured immediately.

Parvovirus is a highly contagious and often fatal intestinal disease characterized by severe vomiting and diarrhea that is often bloody, a high temperature, and rapid dehydration. Although usually preceded by lethargy and loss of appetite, the onset is sudden, and veterinary treatment must be sought at the first sign of symptoms. A preventive vaccine affords protection but must, of course, be given before symptoms appear. **Coronavirus** causes a similar, serious intestinal disease. Both can be prevented by immunization.

Rabies is a disease that is always fatal, and it is transmissible to man. It is caused by a virus that attacks the nervous system and is present in the saliva of an infected animal. When an infected animal bites another, the virus is transmitted to the new victim. It may also enter the body through cuts and scratches that come in contact with saliva containing the virus.

All warm-blooded animals are subject to rabies, and it may be transmitted by foxes, skunks, squirrels, raccoons, horses, and cattle, as well as dogs. Anyone bit by a dog or any other animal should see a physician immediately, and health and law-enforcement officials should be notified. Also, if your dog is bitten by another animal, consult your veterinarian immediately.

In most areas, rabies immunization is required by law. Even if not required, all dogs should be given antirabies vaccine, for it is an effective preventive measure.

DIETARY DEFICIENCY DISEASES

Rickets afflicts puppies not provided with sufficient calcium and vitamin D. Symptoms include lameness, arching of the neck and the back, and a tendency of the legs to bow. Treatment consists of providing adequate amounts of dicalcium phosphate and vitamin D and exposing the dog to sunlight. If the disease is detected and treated before reaching an advanced stage, bone damage may be lessened somewhat, although it cannot be corrected completely.

Osteomalacia, similar to rickets, may occur in adult dogs. Treatment is the same as for rickets, but here, too, prevention is preferable to cure. Permanent deformities resulting from rickets or osteomalacia will not be inherited, so once the victim recovers, he can be used for breeding.

EXTERNAL PARASITES

Fleas, lice, mites, and ticks can be eradicated in your dog's quarters by regular use of an insecticide spray with a four- to six-week residual effect. Bedding, blankets, and pillows should be laundered frequently and treated with an insecticide. Treatment for external parasites varies, depending upon the parasites involved, but a number of good dips and powders are available.

Fleas may be eliminated by dusting the coat thoroughly with flea powder at frequent intervals during the summer months when fleas are a problem.

Flea collars are very effective in keeping a dog free of fleas. Some animals are allergic to the chemicals in the collars, however, so be cautious when you use the collar and check the skin of the neck area frequently. Remove the collar if the skin becomes irritated. Also be careful that the collar is not fastened too tightly. Cut off excess at the end to prevent your dog from chewing it. Remove the collar if it becomes wet or damp, and always remove it before your dog is bathed. Do not replace it around your dog's neck until his coat is completely dry. If your dog reacts to the flea collar, you can hang a medallion from his regular collar. This will eliminate direct skin contact and thus avoid allergic reaction. The medallion should, of course, be removed when the dog is bathed.

Lice may be eradicated by applying dips formulated especially for this purpose to the dog's coat. Use a fine-toothed comb to remove dead lice and eggs, which are firmly attached to the coat.

Mites live deep in the ear canal, producing irritation to the lining of the ear

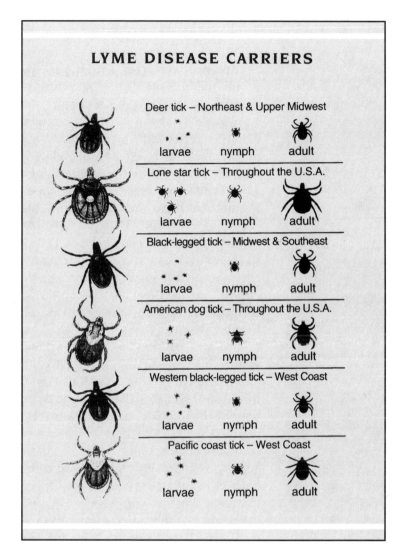

LYME DISEASE CARRIERS

Deer tick – Northeast & Upper Midwest
larvae nymph adult

Lone star tick – Throughout the U.S.A.
larvae nymph adult

Black-legged tick – Midwest & Southeast
larvae nymph adult

American dog tick – Throughout the U.S.A.
larvae nymph adult

Western black-legged tick – West Coast
larvae nymph adult

Pacific coast tick – West Coast
larvae nymph adult

and causing a brownish-black, dry-type discharge. Swab plain mineral oil or ear ointment on the inner surface of the ear twice a week until the mites are eliminated.

Ticks may carry Rocky Mountain spotted fever and Lyme disease. To avoid possible infection, they should be removed from the dog only with tweezers and should be destroyed by burning or by dropping them in insecticide. Heavy infestation can be controlled by sponging the coat daily with a solution containing a special tick dip.

Among other preparations available for controlling parasites on your dog's body are some that can be given internally. Because dosage must be carefully controlled, these preparations should not be used without consulting a veterinarian.

INTERNAL PARASITES

Internal parasites, with the exception of the tapeworm, may be transmitted from a mother dog to her puppies. Infestation may also result from contact with infected bedding or through access to a yard where an infected dog relieves himself. The types that may infest dogs are roundworms, whipworms, tapeworms, hookworms, and heartworms. All cause similar symptoms: a generally unhealthy appearance, stary coat, dull eyes, weakness and emaciation despite a ravenous appetite, coughing, vomiting, diarrhea, and sometimes bloody stools. Not all symptoms are present in every case, of course.

A heavy infestation with any type of worm is a serious matter, and treatment must be started early and continued until the dog is free of the parasite or the dog's health will suffer seriously. Death may even result.

Promiscuous dosing for worms is dangerous, and different types of worms require different treatment. If you suspect that your dog has worms, consult your veterinarian so that a microscopic examination can be made of the feces, and appropriate treatment can be undertaken if an infestation is found.

Heartworms, once thought to be a problem confined to the southern part of the United States, today represent a life-threatening danger to dogs in all parts of the country. Heartworm larvae are transmitted from dog to dog through the bite of the mosquito. Once the larvae have entered the bloodstream, heartworms mature in the heart, where they interfere with heart action, causing chronic coughing and labored breathing.

The tiny heartworm larvae, called microfilariae, can be detected only through a microscopic examination of the dog's blood. Effective preventive medication is available but can be given only if the microscopic examination shows that no microfilaria are present. While medication is also available for treating infested dogs, the degree of success to be expected depends upon the amount of damage already sustained.

Because of the radical nature of the treatment required once infestation occurs, prevention is by far the preferred approach. A veterinarian should be consulted and the advice followed implicitly.

Hookworms are found in puppies as well as in adult dogs. When excreted in the feces, the mature worm looks like a thread and is about three-quarters of an inch in length. Eradication is difficult in areas where the soil is infested with the worms, because the dog may then become reinfested after treatment. Consequently, medication usually must be repeated at intervals, and the premises, including the grounds where the dog exercises, must be treated and kept well drained.

Roundworms are the most common of all worms that may infest a dog, because most puppies are born with them or become infested with them shortly after birth. Roundworms vary in length from two to eight inches and can be detected readily through a microscopic examination of the feces. At maturity, upon excretion, the roundworm will spiral into a circle, but after it dies, it resembles a cut rubber band.

If you suspect that your puppy has roundworms, check his gums and tongue. If the puppy is heavily infested, the worms will cause anemia and the gums and the tongue will be very pale pink in color. If the puppy is anemic, the veterinarian will probably prescribe a tonic in addition to the proper worm medicine.

Tapeworms require an intermediate host, usually the flea or the louse, but they sometimes are found in raw fish. A dog can therefore become infested by swallowing a flea or a louse, or by eating infested fish.

A complete tapeworm can be two to three feet long. The head and neck of the tapeworm are small and threadlike, while the body is made up of segments like links of a sausage, which are about half an inch long and flat. Segments of the body separate from the worm and are found in the

LIFE CYCLE OF THE HEARTWORM

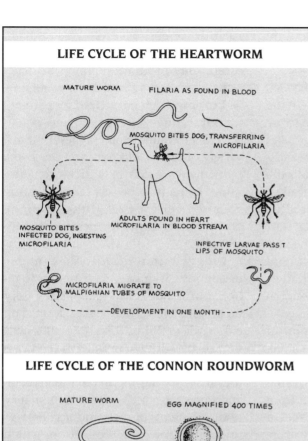

LIFE CYCLE OF THE FLEA HOST TAPEWORM

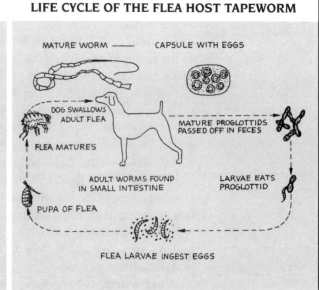

LIFE CYCLE OF THE CONNON ROUNDWORM

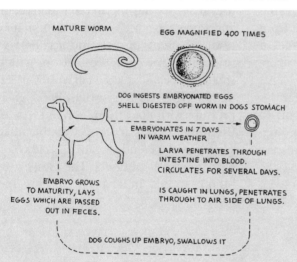

LIFE CYCLE OF THE WHIPWORM

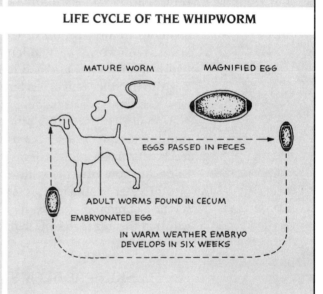

LIFE CYCLE OF THE HOOKWORM

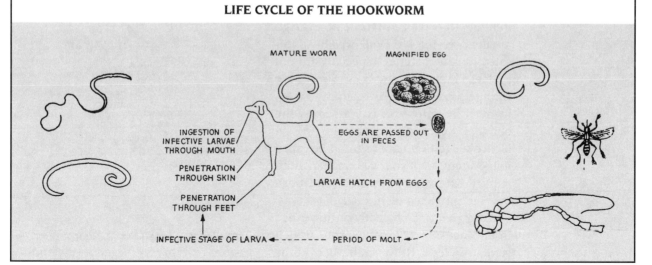

feces or will hang from the coat around the anus. When dry, they resemble dark grains of rice.

The head of the tapeworm is imbedded in the lining of the intestine, where the worm feeds on the blood of the dog. The difficulty in eradicating the tapeworm lies in the fact that most medicines have a laxative action that is too severe. It pulls the body of the tapeworm from the head so that the body is eliminated with the feces, but the implanted head remains to start growing a new body. An effective medication is a tablet that does not dissolve until it reaches the intestine, where it anesthetizes the worm and loosens its head so that it can be expelled.

Whipworms are more common in the eastern states than in the states along the West Coast, but whipworms may infest dogs in any section of the United States. Whipworms vary in length from two to four inches and are tapered in shape so that they resemble a buggy whip, which accounts for its name.

At maturity, the whipworm migrates into the cecum, where it is difficult to reach with medication. A fecal examination will show whether whipworms are present. After treatment, it is best to have several examinations made in order to be sure that the dog is free of them.

SKIN PROBLEMS

Skin problems usually cause persistent itching. However, **follicular mange** usually does not. It is evidenced by moth-eaten-looking patches, especially around the head and along the back. **Sarcoptic mange** produces severe itching and is evidenced by patchy, crusty areas on the body, the legs, and the abdomen. Any evidence suggesting either should be called to the attention of your veterinarian. Both require extensive treatment, and both may be contracted by humans.

Allergies are not readily distinguished from other skin troubles except through laboratory tests. However, be alert to the fact that various coat dressings and shampoos, or simply bathing your dog too often, may produce allergic skin reactions.

Eczema is characterized by extreme itching, redness of the skin, and exudation of serous matter. It may result from a variety of causes, but the exact cause in a particular case may be difficult to determine. Relief may be secured by dusting your dog twice a week with a soothing powder containing a fungicide and an insecticide.

Clogged anal glands cause intense discomfort. Your dog may attempt to relieve himself by scooting along the floor on his haunches. These glands, located on either side of the anus, secrete a substance that enables the dog to expel the contents of the rectum. If they become clogged, they may give the dog an unpleasant odor, and when neglected, serious infection may result. Contents of the glands can be easily expelled into a wad of cotton, which should be held under the tail with your left hand. Then, using your right hand, exert pressure with your thumb on one side of the anus and your forefinger on the other. The normal secretion is brownish in color, with an unpleasant odor. The presence of blood or pus indicates infection and

This illustration shows the correct procedure to express clogged anal glands.

should be called to the attention of your veterinarian.

Eye problems of a minor nature, such as redness or occasional discharge, may be treated with a few drops of boric-acid solution (2 percent) or salt solution (one teaspoon of table salt to one pint of sterile water). Cuts on the eyeball, bruises close to the eyes, or persistent discharge should be treated only by a veterinarian.

Heat exhaustion is a serious and often fatal problem caused by exposure to extreme heat. Usually it occurs when a thoughtless owner leaves the dog in a closed vehicle without proper shade and ventilation. Even on a day when outside temperatures do not seem excessively high, heat builds up rapidly to an extremely high temperature in a closed vehicle parked in direct sunlight or even in partial shade. Many dogs and young children die each year from being left in an inadequately ventilated vehicle. To prevent such a tragedy, never leave a dog or child unattended in a vehicle even for a short period of time.

During hot weather, whenever you take your dog for a ride in an air-conditioned automobile, reduce the cool air gradually when nearing your destination, because the sudden shock of going from cool air to extremely hot temperatures can also result in shock and heat exhaustion.

Symptoms of heat exhaustion include rapid and difficult breathing and near or complete collapse. After removing the victim from the vehicle, first-aid treatment consists of sponging cool water over the body to reduce the temperature as quickly as possible. Immediate medical treatment is essential in severe cases of heat exhaustion.

CARE OF THE AILING OR INJURED DOG

A dog that is seriously ill, requiring surgical treatment, transfusions, or intravenous feeding, must be hospitalized. One requiring less complicated treatment is better cared for at home, but it is essential that the dog be kept in a quiet environment. Preferably his bed should be in a room apart from family activity, yet close at hand so that his condition can be checked frequently. Clean bedding and adequate warmth are essential, as are a constant supply of fresh, cool water, and foods to tempt the appetite.

If special medication is prescribed, it may be administered in any of several ways. A pill or small capsule may be concealed in a small piece of meat, which the dog will usually swallow with no problem. A large capsule may be given by holding your dog's mouth open, inserting the capsule as far as possible down the throat, then holding the mouth closed until the dog swallows. Liquid medicine should be measured into a small bottle or test tube. Then, if the corner of the dog's lip is pulled out while the head is tilted upward, the liquid can be poured between the lips and the teeth, a small amount at a time. If he refuses to swallow, keeping the dog's head tilted and stroking his throat will usually induce swallowing.

Liquid medication may also be given by use of a hypodermic syringe without a needle attached. The syringe is slipped into the side of the mouth and over the rise at the back of the tongue, and the medicine is "injected" slowly down the throat. This is especially good for medicine with a bad taste, because the medicine does not touch the taste buds in the front part of the tongue. It also eliminates spills and guarantees that all of the medicine goes in.

Foods offered the sick dog should be nutritious and easily digested. Meals should be smaller than usual and offered at more frequent intervals. If your dog is reluctant to eat, offer the food he particularly likes. Warm it slightly to increase the aroma and make it more tempting.

GENETIC DISEASES

There are a number of diseases that affect the Labrador Retriever. These are genetic

THE FIRST AID KIT

The following items should be kept on hand for caring for a sick or injured dog or for administering first aid for injuries:

- Petroleum jelly
- Hydrogen peroxide (for wound cleaning or to induce vomiting)
- Cotton balls, cotton swabs, gauze pads, and gauze wraps
- Rectal thermometer
- Tweezers
- Several syringes without needles
- Measuring spoons or container for liquid medication
- Adhesive tape and stretch bandages
- Burn ointment
- Panalog or triple antiseptic ointment
- Bag balm
- Boric acid solution (2%) or a commercial pet eye wash
- Surgical shampoo such as Betadine
- Small forceps
- Kaopectate or Pepto-Bismol
- Baby aspirin

diseases and as such are inherited and are passed from one generation to the next. These diseases can be classified as genetically dominant or recessive. These classifications were established by Gregor J. Mendel, the nineteenth-century Austrian botanist. Under Mendel's Law, dominant characteristics predominate over recessive characteristics. The two diseases of the Labrador Retriever that are considered dominant are bilateral cataracts and central progressive retinal atrophy. Other diseases that are considered recessive are carpal subluxation, cystinuria, hemophilia A, myopathy, and retinal dysplasia.

Hungarian import Ch. Atokhazi Anonymus, owned by Carole J. Nickerson.

SPECIFIC GENETIC DISEASES

Carpal subluxation is an incomplete dislocation of the carpal or wrist bones. This is not a common condition. When present, it can be identified by steeply slanted pasterns.

Cataracts refer to the opacity of the lens. This condition can normally be identified by a milky white spot on the eyeball. This may be a small spot or may cover the entire surface of the eyeball. Cataracts can appear as early as one year of age, but they are more common in older animals. Many dogs older than eight or nine years have some cloudiness to the lens. Diabetes is sometimes accompanied by cataracts.

Colobama is a condition of the eye that is seen occasionally. This describes a condition of the iris or the eyelid in which a fissure appears. In the iris it is inferior, and in the eyelid it is superior.

Craniomandibular osteopathy is a disease of the bone of the lower jaw—the mandible. This disease results in a thickening of this bone.

Cystinuria is a disease of the renal system in which the reabsorption of certain minerals is inhibited, resulting in the formation of stones.

Dacrocystitis is an inflammation of the lachrymal sac and compromises the tear duct.

Diabetes is a disease that results when the pancreas does not function in a normal fashion. The insulin mechanism is compromised, resulting in a disorder of carbohydrate metabolism and hyperglycemia. This condition is manifested by an extreme thirst and the passing of excessive quantities of urine.

Distichiasis describes the condition of the eyelid when a second row of eyelashes appears. This extra row is on the inner lid of the eye and rubs directly on the cornea, damaging the surface of the cornea.

Ectropian describes the condition of the lower eyelid when the muscle is weak and the eyelid itself is loose. This can result in a haw. For a Labrador Retriever working in the field, where seeds and dust are always present, this could cause a serious problem.

Entropian is an inversion or turning in of the eyelid that causes the eyelashes to rub against the cornea. The result is the same as in distichiasis, but in this case there is not an extra row of eyelashes.

Epilepsy results when there is an excessive and uncontrolled discharge of neurons in the brain. The result is a malfunction of motor and sensory behavior. This condition is manifested by tremors, seizures, and convulsions. Medications can be very effective in treating some types of epilepsy.

Hemophilia A describes a condition of the blood that results in internal bleeding. This is usually seen in male Labrador Retrievers, although it is carried genetically by the female. In dogs with this condition there is a deficiency of Factor VIII, which helps to control the coagulation of the blood. This condition was present in

Ch. Baroke Yellow Jacket. Photo by Keith Grimson.

the family of the Russian Tsars in the nineteenth century.

Hip dysplasia is a disease of the hip joint that occurs when the fit between the head of the femur and the acetabulum of the pelvis deteriorates. The femur slips out of its normal position in the acetabulum, and the hip becomes dislocated. This condition is seen mainly in the larger, heavier dogs; it is not common in dogs weighing less than thirty pounds. The disease is progressive and can eventually cripple an older dog. There are two X-ray tests that can detect this condition. One is governed by the Orthopedic Foundation for Animals (OFA) and the second, called the Penn-Hip test, is conducted by the University of Pennsylvania School of Veterinary Medicine. The Penn-Hip test can be used on younger dogs. This is valuable, because the condition can be detected before the dog is used for breeding.

Hypertropic osteodystrophy describes the defective development of bone in the young dog. This can result in a ricketslike condition or in dwarfism.

Hypoglycemia is an abnormally low level of glucose or sugar in the blood.

Ch. Golden Chance of Franklin, owned by Mrs. B.W. Ziessow. Photo by Frasie.

When this condition reaches a critical level, the dog can go into convulsions.

Myopathy is any disease of the muscle. There are numerous possibilities for the dysfunction of a muscle. They govern the way that a dog moves or behaves, because he can no longer function as he did in the past. When muscular atrophy occurs in older dogs and they cannot move as freely as they did when they were young, they become more sedentary. The gait in a dog of any age can be affected by compromised muscles. The gait can become stilted or choppy with a bouncing top line and a bobbing of the head. The particular conditions determine what treatment, if any, will be effective.

Osteochondritis dissecans results when the articular cartilage is either partially or completely detached from the bone. In humans it is often described as "football player's knee."

Progressive retinal atrophy, or PRA, is a condition usually found in older dogs. It is characterized by a degeneration of the cells of the retina, which eventually leads to blindness. The first manifestation of the disease is night blindness, resulting in the dog's not wanting to go into dark areas because he can no longer distinguish objects.

Central progressive retinal atrophy is confined to the center of the eye, which makes it difficult for the dog to see stationary objects in front of him. Peripheral vision still exists, so moving objects can still be tracked.

Retinal dysplasia is a condition present at birth and is a defect of the inner layer of the optic vesicle. This compromises the pigment and sensory functioning of the retina.

Von Willibrand's disease describes vascular hemophilia. Excessive and unanticipated internal bleeding can occur in dogs with this condition. A slight injury or even stress can bring on an attack.

CONDITIONING YOUR LABRADOR RETRIEVER

Whether your Labrador Retriever is a show dog, a field dog, or a family pet, his conditioning is extremely important. Being a large dog, he will need quantity as well as high-quality food. Because the key to proper conditioning is the basic diet of your dog, maintain a well-balanced diet at all times. Meals can be varied to make them interesting without sacrificing standards of nutrition, and vitamin and mineral supplements can be added.

A healthy coat can be maintained only with proper nutrition. A dog cannot grow the correct coat unless he is fed a well-balanced diet. To produce such a coat, a Labrador Retriever must gain and maintain the weight consistent with his size. Many Labrador Retrievers will overeat if given the opportunity. While the overly fat dog may be accepted as a family pet, he cannot be accepted as a show dog and will not perform well in the field. Because of the ease with which a Labrador Retriever gains weight, his food must be measured. The quantity of food can be increased with increased exercise, but the dog's weight should be checked regularly to prevent unwanted gains.

In addition to a well-balanced diet, proper exercise is necessary for all dogs. An hour or two each day should be set aside to exercise your dog. If your dog is the family pet, allow him to romp in a fenced area or take him for a walk. A well-drained run covered with three or four inches of gravel is easy to keep clean and will keep your dog out of the mud on rainy days. An occasional lime treatment eliminates odors. Dry lime can be sprinkled over the surface and then thoroughly washed through with a hose to prevent your dog from picking it up on the pads of his feet.

Labrador Retrievers need more exercise than many other breeds in order to stay in top shape and to maintain the correct

Ch. Baroke Cindy, owned by Keith S. Grimson of Baroke Kennels. Field work is good exercise.

muscle tone. When Labrador Retrievers are allowed to run with another active dog in a large, fenced area, they are able to get the necessary exercise. However, when a Labrador Retriever is alone, he will need some structured exercise in order to maintain muscle tone. Jogging or running beside a bicycle are two ways to exercise your Lab.

Regulated exercise is important not only for the working Labrador Retriever, but also for the show dog. A dog that is underexercised will not gait properly and cannot possibly maintain the necessary balance of muscle to bone. A carefully structured training program should be established and adhered to in order to keep your dog in prime condition.

The show Labrador Retriever should be trained in showring pattern drills while he is still very young so that they will become

Body condition chart. Maintaning your Labrador Retriever at his optimum weight and body condition is one of the best things you can do for his overall good health. Reprinted with permission from Purina Mills.

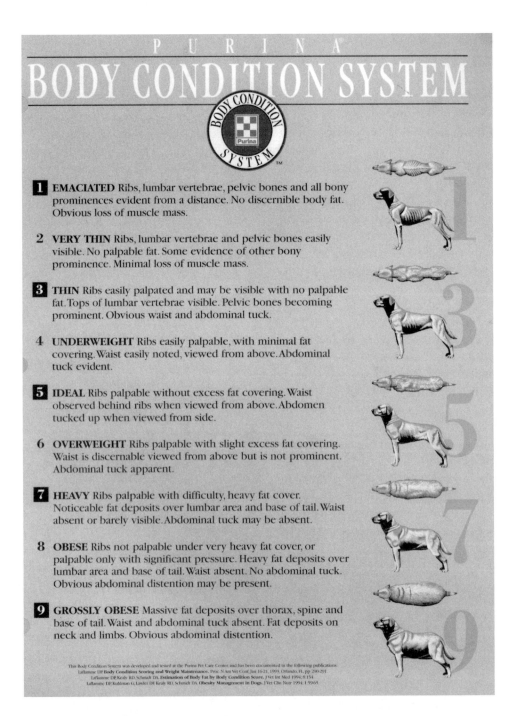

PURINA
BODY CONDITION SYSTEM

1 EMACIATED Ribs, lumbar vertebrae, pelvic bones and all bony prominences evident from a distance. No discernible body fat. Obvious loss of muscle mass.

2 VERY THIN Ribs, lumbar vertebrae and pelvic bones easily visible. No palpable fat. Some evidence of other bony prominence. Minimal loss of muscle mass.

3 THIN Ribs easily palpated and may be visible with no palpable fat. Tops of lumbar vertebrae visible. Pelvic bones becoming prominent. Obvious waist and abdominal tuck.

4 UNDERWEIGHT Ribs easily palpable, with minimal fat covering. Waist easily noted, viewed from above. Abdominal tuck evident.

5 IDEAL Ribs palpable without excess fat covering. Waist observed behind ribs when viewed from above. Abdomen tucked up when viewed from side.

6 OVERWEIGHT Ribs palpable with slight excess fat covering. Waist is discernable viewed from above but is not prominent. Abdominal tuck apparent.

7 HEAVY Ribs palpable with difficulty, heavy fat cover. Noticeable fat deposits over lumbar area and base of tail. Waist absent or barely visible. Abdominal tuck may be absent.

8 OBESE Ribs not palpable under very heavy fat cover, or palpable only with significant pressure. Heavy fat deposits over lumbar area and base of tail. Waist absent. No abdominal tuck. Obvious abdominal distention may be present.

9 GROSSLY OBESE Massive fat deposits over thorax, spine and base of tail. Waist and abdominal tuck absent. Fat deposits on neck and limbs. Obvious abdominal distention.

This Body Condition System was developed and tested at the Purina Pet Care Center and has been documented in the following publications:
Laflamme DP. Body Condition Scoring and Weight Maintenance. Proc N Am Vet Conf Jan 16-21, 1995, Orlando, FL, pp 290-291
Laflamme DP, Kealy RD, Schmidt DA. Estimation of Body Fat by Body Condition Score. J Vet Int Med 1994; 8:154
Laflamme DP, Kuhlman G, Lawler DF, Kealy RD, Schmidt DA. Obesity Management in Dogs. J Vet Clin Nutr 1994; 1:5965.

a part of his routine. He should be taught the correct show pose and trained to hold this pose for the proper length of time. With this training, he develops the necessary self-discipline to stand for the examination of the judge.

When your puppy is just a few weeks old, set him up in a show pose. Place his feet correctly so that he gets the feel of this position. If the puppy moves his feet, reset them with a gentle but firm action. Set his foot by grasping the leg above the elbow joint. This allows you to control not only the position of the foot, but the whole leg as well. This assures that your dog will be in a solid, comfortable position that cannot be achieved merely by twisting his foot. If the foot is not solidly placed, the dog will lean for balance. This will *not* be to his advantage.

COAT CARE

Establish a regular schedule of bathing and grooming early in your puppy's life so that you are always well ahead of any coat problem that might arise. Brushing with a slicker brush or grooming mitt should start while the puppy is only a few weeks old. His coat will need very little real attention at this age, but this early schedule will help train him for some of the longer grooming sessions that will follow at a later date. The easiest way to start training is to brush the puppy gently while holding him in your lap.

To be healthy, a coat must be clean. A coat that is allowed to become dirty will tangle quickly and may develop small mats. If the coat is dirty, sticky, or caked with mud, which is sometimes the case when the dog is allowed to run freely in the field, the dog should be bathed thoroughly before an attempt is made to brush him. A partial bath or even a partial rinsing will sometimes suffice.

The Labrador Retriever changes coat with the seasons. In the late spring, he will shed his winter undercoat prior to growing a new healthy summer coat. During this time, the coat should be brushed

Show training should start early for a future champion! Royal Flush has already learned enough discipline to hold a show pose with only his tail being held.

EXERCISE CHOICES FOR YOUR LABRADOR

- Play ball. Teach your dog to retrieve.
- Throw a Frisbee, canvas disk, or Go-Frrrs toy.
- Take him for a swim in the lake.
- Toss a floating object for him to retrieve from the water.
- Take your dog for a hike in the hills.
- Jog around the neighborhood with your dog, or consider entering a race for dogs and their owners.
- Let the kids romp, roll, and tumble with him.
- Take your dog along on a bike ride.
- Take him hunting.
- Give him a treat ball filled with goodies so he exercises himself while you're away.
- Allow free time in a dog run or your backyard, preferably with another dog.
- Install a dog door so he can come and go into the yard at will.
- Take him for a romp at the park and let him romp on a long Flexi lead.
- Teach him to jump or do agility.
- Get involved in an active sport like tracking, field trials, or retriever tests.

Swimming and playing with another dog are excellent activities to keep your Labrador fit. Photo © Karen Hudson.

thoroughly every day. The old dead hair must be removed to allow the new coat to come in. This regular brushing stimulates the hair follicles and aids new hair growth. A second change of coat occurs in the fall, but this is of less consequence than the spring blowing of undercoat.

CONDITIONING FOR THE SHOWRING

The Labrador Retriever is a natural dog and requires only limited grooming to make him ready for the ring. Trim the hair from between his pads to increase his traction as he gaits in the ring. Trim his nails weekly and keep them as short as possible. You may trim the whiskers and eyebrows even with the skin. Labrador Retrievers seem to have a knack for pulling in their whiskers during trimming. Sliding your finger under his lip helps hold the whiskers out and facilitates cutting them. The final step in readying your dog for the showring is to spray his coat with coat dressing and rub it dry with either a grooming mitt or a bristle brush.

When you are at a show and your class is called, you already should have determined where your dog will show to the best advantage, and you should try to get in that place in line if you can accomplish it tactfully. If your dog gaits rapidly, the head of the line would be the preferred position. If he moves slowly, however, the end of the line is the obvious choice. A slow-moving dog in the middle of the line only calls attention to the fact that he does not move well. The end of the line is also the best place to show a dog that in other positions keeps looking back at the dog following him. Take advantage of techniques that will show your dog to the best advantage. Remember, however, that a competent judge will find the best dog no matter where he is in line as long as he is shown to advantage.

Most Labrador Retrievers are natural showmen in the ring and will need very little corrective positioning. This will be especially true if your dog has been trained to pose as a puppy. He will gait easily and freely and will stop four-square if he is not caught off stride. If your dog stops off balance, take an additional step. This will allow your dog to correct his pose. Another technique to correct an off-balance pose is to pull lightly on the lead so that the dog will lean away from the weight-carrying leg. This will bring him to his natural pose.

When you set up your dog for the judge's examination, it may be necessary to pose each leg individually. The matting in the ring is not a normal place for a dog, and he may feel uncomfortable the first few times. To aid in the training of a puppy, it would be a good idea to purchase a piece of rubber show matting and practice with this at home before ever going to a show. Positioning each leg solidly gives the dog a feeling of security and allows him to be seen to his best advantage.

In the ring, the dog should be set up and then worked just enough to keep him in pose. Overhandling a dog tends to make him nervous and prevents the judge

Ch. Driftwood's Rusty of Ro-Shan, owned by Tom and Phyllis Philip of Ro-Shan Kennels.

from getting a good look at him. Remember that a judge is always looking at your dog. Even if the judge is at the other end of the line, he may glance back to see how your dog looks in comparison to the one he is examining. Allowing your dog to sit or sag can lose a placement.

Obviously, there is no perfect dog, because every dog has strong points and weak points. Consequently, the strong points should be emphasized and the weak ones minimized. This is not unethical, because all exhibitors must contend with similar difficulties. The judge will pick the best dog in the class, and you must prove that your dog has more strong qualities than the other dogs in the ring. The judge selects the best one present that particular day in comparison with the other entries.

Puppy classes are excellent for socializing and conditioning puppies. Here a Lab puppy is encouraged to scale a small "A frame" as part of his puppy class exercises. Photo by B. J. McKinney.

Ch. Triple L's Coral Ridge at the end of a successful hunting day.

chapter nine

FIELD TRIALS AND HUNTING TESTS

Labrador Retriever owners and trainers are quick to see the retrieving instinct and competitive nature of the breed as their dog matures. These traits become obvious as you watch your puppy carry around anything that he can get into his mouth. It may be a stick, a tennis ball, or a puppy training bumper, but the puppy seems to be genuinely proud of his accomplishment. The retrieving instinct becomes more pronounced as the puppy grows, and it is not unusual for you to want to develop your dog's natural abilities for the field and for competition at organized field trials or hunting tests. With persistence and patience in training, and with help from books, videos, and especially other people who have trained retriever breeds, you may in time produce a Labrador Retriever that will be a fine hunting companion and also competitive in field trials and hunting tests. To provide organized competition among retrieving-dog enthusiasts, retriever clubs have developed across the United States and Canada.

RETRIEVER CLUBS AND PROGRAMS

The first retrieving-dog event was held in 1932, and since that time the sport has developed significantly. There are more than 120 field-trial clubs in the United States today. Most of these clubs sponsor retriever trials or hunting tests that are run under the direction of the AKC, but other organizations such as the Hunting Retriever Club, Inc., working with the United Kennel Club, Inc., also provide tests for the hunting retriever. The AKC, in consultation with the Retriever Advisory Committee (composed of delegates from member retriever clubs), provides guidelines and regulations that ensure greater uniformity in competition and in judging the performances of retrievers. Guidelines for field trials are found in a booklet entitled *Registration and Field Trial Rules and Standard Procedure for Retrievers* including *Standing Recommendations of the Retriever Advisory Committee* and the *Supplement to the Standard Procedure*. It was amended on September 1, 1993 and contains important information for the organization and judging of retriever trials. If you want to train your Labrador Retriever for field competition, you should become familiar with Chapter 17, Rules for Retriever Trials, and especially Part II, Evaluation of Dog Work. Copies are available from the AKC. You may also access the AKC through the Internet at http://www.akc.org/akc/. Revisions to the rules and regulations are made periodically by the Retriever Advisory Committee to keep pace with the sport.

MHR American and Canadian Ch. Plantier's Ruthless Ruthie, C.D., M.H., owner Dick Plantier.

In 1985, the AKC began a program for hunting retrievers and developed a set of regulations and guidelines that can be found in another AKC publication entitled *Regulations and Guidelines for AKC Hunting Tests for Retrievers* (also available from the AKC). The purpose of these tests is to allow the hunting retriever to be evaluated against a set of standards that more closely simulate actual hunting conditions. These tests are not necessarily intended to replace the AKC's field trials for retrievers, but rather to complement them. These events test the abilities of retrievers that serve primarily as hunting companions.

All dogs entered in a field trial or hunting test must be AKC registered or from an AKC-registered litter. Only breeds listed as retrievers by the AKC are eligible for retriever trials. The three retrieving breeds that are the most popular are Labrador Retrievers, Golden Retrievers, and Chesapeake Bay Retrievers. Other breeds eligible for the trials are Flat-Coated Retrievers, Irish Water Spaniels, and Curly-Coated Retrievers.

Retriever clubs, depending on their affiliation, may hold or sponsor trials or hunting tests. A club or association that is a member of the AKC may sponsor a member field trial or hunting test at which championship points are awarded. A club or association may receive a special license to sponsor a licensed field trial or hunting test. Championship points are also awarded at these trials. Nonaffiliated clubs may sponsor a sanctioned (or informal) field trial or hunting test, where championship points are not awarded. Sanctioned events, however, do give both handler and dog experience under actual field and competition conditions.

Retriever clubs always welcome new members and guests and actively solicit participation in club activities. These clubs not only provide you with access to people with a lot of retriever-training knowledge, they also serve as a social outlet. Many of the members first became interested in the club because they found the Labrador Retriever to be an excellent friend and hunting companion and want-

Campbellcroft's Banks, J.H., owned by Donald and Virginia Campbell.

Jazztime's Alaskan Rendezvous and FC, AFC, CFC, CAFC, MHR Jazztime, owned by Larry and Anna Calvert.

ed to become involved with others with similar experiences and interests.

Clubs frequently have fun trials, where dogs and handlers compete under less rigorous conditions than seen in the member and licensed field trials. Awards are usually presented to the winners, and club champions may be selected. In addition, numerous training sessions are sponsored by the club throughout the year. These provide excellent opportunities for the novice to find help and advice. Other topics frequently arise, such as: What is the best size shot to use on doves? What choke should be used on upland game? What duck decoy placement is best for mallards? Some of the best times you will experience will be when you stand around in the field after a productive training session talking to your retriever-training friends.

Membership in a field club is definitely advantageous to the beginner, because within the club membership you find individuals with expert knowledge both of accepted methods of retriever training and of the mechanics of field trials and hunting tests. You can find out about such clubs

in the *Retriever Field Trial News,* a monthly periodical containing information about retriever breeds, owned and sponsored by the National Retriever Club and the National Amateur Retriever Club. It lists dates and locations of AKC-licensed and member club events and results, as well as other valuable information related to Labrador Retrievers and the other retrieving breeds. The name and address of the secretary of each retriever club is frequently listed so that a club member may be contacted for information. Licensed and member trials are also listed in the *AKC Gazette,* the official publication of the AKC.

FIELD AND HUNTING EVENTS

Field trials and hunting tests are staged in areas that best simulate actual hunting conditions. Managed wildlife areas, other public lands, and private grounds make excellent running grounds and are readily accessible by automobile. Signs are posted along the roads by the sponsoring club to direct people to the trial areas. The

FC and AFC Barracuda Blue, owned by Charles and Missy Tyson.

Ch. Campbellcroft's Top Dwarer, C.D., J.H., W.C., owned by Donald Campbell.

spectators, or gallery, are positioned so as not to interfere with the handler or dog. Participants or others in the gallery are happy to explain the proceedings to first-time spectators. Most beginners become enthusiastic and more serious about training their dog after having attended a field trial or hunting test.

The event is composed of different classes or stakes, and the number of entries will vary. Entering your dog in competition requires you to decide carefully on which stake to enter. The choice depends entirely upon the maturity and the stage of training of your dog, and each stake is run to provide dogs, regardless of the level of training, a place to compete.

In a field trial, the Derby Stake is for dogs that are older than six months of age and not yet two years of age on the first day of the trial at which they are being run. This stake is for the young dog, and judging is based on traits such as desire, style, and speed, as well as performance. The Qualifying Stake is for dogs older than six months of age that have never won a first, second, third, or fourth place or a Judges' Award of Merit (JAM) in an Open All-Age, Limited All-Age, or Special All-Age Stake; a first, second, third, or fourth place in an Amateur All-Age Stake; or two first places in Qualifying Stakes. This stake is an intermediate category. The advanced dog is rarely entered, and it is not uncommon to find the hunter and his companion dog among the competitors in the Qualifying. The tests, however, are difficult, and you should expect stiff competition.

The Amateur All-Age Stake is for any dog older than six months of age, if handled in that stake by an amateur. This is a very popular stake and is usually well attended. Entries are limited to amateur trainers who do not train retrievers professionally. The competition in this class is excellent, the tests are difficult, and only well-trained dogs should be entered. The Open All-Age Stake is for any dog older than six months of age, but because this class is the most difficult in terms of competition, only the most seasoned dogs should be entered. Professional handlers compete here.

Two other stakes are the Limited All-Age and the Special All-Age. The Limited All-Age is for dogs that have been placed or that have received a JAM in a licensed Open or Amateur Stake or that have received a first or second in a Qualifying Stake. The Special All-Age Stake is for dogs that have been awarded points or a JAM during the current or previous calendar year.

Championships are awarded in the Amateur and Open stakes. After judging to determine the best of the field, dogs are placed as first, second, third, and fourth. No other placement is announced. This placement is determined by the judges after all dogs have been run in several series to show both natural and acquired abilities. Five points are awarded for first place, three points for second, one point for third and one-half point for fourth. To acquire an Amateur Field Championship (AFC), the dog must have accumulated a total of fifteen points and must have taken a first place in at least one trial. To be awarded the title of Field Champion (FC), the dog must have acquired ten points and must have taken first place in at least one Open stake.

In hunting tests, qualifying scores are awarded when the dog meets certain judging standards. Three groups or classes are awarded points: Junior, Senior, and Master. The complexity of the tests increases from Junior to Master. The tests are designed to assess basically the same abilities of dogs entered in AKC field trials. However, in hunting tests, the dog is evaluated against a hunting standard, and the test more closely simulates a hunting condition. The other difference is that dogs finishing a hunting test are not ranked on a numerical score. The dog receives a numerical score on a scale of zero to ten in each ability category but is not ranked with other entrants based on that score. In other words, the dog is competing against a standard, and if the standard is met, the dog receives a score. To receive a

Eneabba, M.H., owned by Dick Weiner.

Can. Ch. West Wind Saila of Cedarwood, Am. and Can. C.D., J.H., A.W.C., C.W.C., C.G.C. co-owned by Dave Robiehaud and Nancy Brandow, and Am. and Can. Ch. Pine Edge Sunnybrook Pebbles, J.H., A.W.C., C.W.C. owned by Nancy Brandow.

1. At a field trial the water retrieve is an important test of the dog's ability.

2. The handler gives the dog the command and the dog moves out.

3. The handler gives the dog a hand signal to move to the right.

4. The judges signal across the lake for an assistant to release the bird. The dog on the left will make the retrieve and the dog on the right will honor him.

5. A gunner downs a bird for the dog to retrieve.

6. The handler, standing in front of the judges, signals the dog in the water to swim to the left.

qualifying score, a dog must have an average of five or more on each ability being evaluated. The dog cannot get a qualifying score if two judges give the dog a zero for a specific ability. An evaluation form is used that lists the abilities tested. This evaluation form may be found in the AKC publication previously mentioned.

To be awarded the Junior Hunter (JH) title, the dog must have qualifying scores in the Junior hunting test in four AKC-licensed or member-club hunting tests. The Senior Hunter (SH) title is given to the dog that has qualifying scores in the Senior Hunting Test at five AKC-licensed or member-club hunting tests. If the dog has been awarded the JH title, only four qualifying scores are required. The Master Hunter (MH) title is awarded after completion of qualifying scores in the Master hunting test at six AKC-licensed or member-club hunting tests. If the dog has an SH title, qualifying scores are required from only five hunting tests.

Club members make a sincere effort to manage field trials and hunting tests so that there is consistency and standardization of objectives from one event to the next. The tests are set up to simulate field conditions that are encountered by the hunter and his dog during an average hunt. Various activities necessary to attain this goal, such as choosing judges, advertising, and preparing premium lists, are managed and coordinated by club members. The end result is the judgment of the performance of the handler and the dog and the placement or awarding of a qualifying score to the best of the field of dogs. At an event, the retriever in general is required to retrieve any fallen game bird, which might include a pigeon, a pheasant, a chukar, a guinea hen, or a duck. The dog is required to walk at heel, sit, and stay at the position designated by the handler. He should retrieve the game when ordered to do so and should do this with purpose and style. The bird should be delivered to the handler, and the dog should then wait for further orders.

According to the AKC, it is the duty of the judges to judge the dogs for their (1) natural abilities and (2) abilities acquired through training. Natural abilities include traits such as memory, intelligence, attention, nose, courage, perseverance, and style. Abilities acquired through training include steadiness, control, response to direction, and delivery. Judges for trials are selected for their knowledge of the breed and their knowledge of superior abilities displayed in the field by individual dogs. The judges set up tests that are intended to assess the abilities of the dog. In the end, the judges select the dogs that perform best under the conditions of the test or that meet certain standards. Meritorious performances are acknowledged by the field-trial judges by placing the best in the field first, second, third, or fourth. Occasionally, a JAM is presented to a dog that performs outstandingly but does not place in the top four. In hunting tests, judges award qualifying scores in ability categories on the basis of a zero-to-ten numerical score. Retrievers entered in either the Amateur or Open Class at AKC field trials accumulate wins and points that qualify them for the National Amateur Championship Stake or the National (Open) Championship Stake. These are special trials held each year and are designed to determine the best dogs from all those entered in trials that particular year.

Retriever field trials and hunting tests are serious events to both the professional and the amateur. The trial is the culmination of months and even years of training. The gallery is able to witness a variety of emotions as the retriever attempts the various tests with both success and failure. Most retriever trainers agree that the competition is beneficial for perpetuation of quality traits in the breed and certainly prepares the gundog for situations commonly encountered in the field.

Perhaps the most important trait seen in the field retriever is the ability to "mark." This term implies the capacity to remember the area where the game has fallen, and the retriever should show accuracy in remembering the position of the fallen bird.

1. The first handler is "on the line" while the second handler is at-the-ready awaiting her turn behind the screen so that her dog cannot see the fall.

2. The judge signals the bird thrower to release the bird. The dog is anticipating the fall.

3. The judges watch while the handler "lines" his dog.

4. The judge calls the dog's number and the handler sends his dog.

This ability is enhanced in the dog that is attentive and anxious to retrieve.

Training methods used during routine sessions can sharpen marking ability, but the basis of this characteristic is inherited. If you are thinking about buying a hunting retriever puppy, ask the breeder about the marking abilities of the puppy's parents and grandparents. Most breeders consider this trait to be of extreme importance in the selection of breeding stock. A large percentage of the tests in a field trial or hunting test stake are contrived to assess marking ability. The degree of difficulty of the mark is a decision made by the judges but will vary depending upon the terrain and the weather conditions. The dog may be required to retrieve on land or water, but often a combination of both. There are always obstacles, such as ditches, tall grass or weeds, plowed fields, or other barriers, to be negotiated, all of which tend to make the mark more difficult. Light conditions, wind, and scenting conditions all play a role each time the dog is required to retrieve.

To provide marks in a field trial or hunting test, hunting conditions are simulated either by having gunners shoot a shotgun into the air as a dead bird is thrown into the air or by having gunners actually shoot live, flighted birds so that they fall into predetermined areas. In hunting tests, you may be required to carry an unloaded shotgun. Dogs are usually more enthusiastic about retrieving actual birds and mark better than when retrieving canvas training bumpers or dummies. The tests become more difficult as the dogs are asked to remember accurately two, three, and perhaps four falls and to retrieve these with a minimum of difficulty. Multiple marks are thrown in succession with time in between so that the dog has a moment to concentrate on the area. It is advantageous for the dog to remember the area of the fall, but the dog that systematically hunts outside this area to find the bird has done a creditable job. The hunting spirit should be manifest in the Labrador Retriever's determination to find the bird, and he may use his intelligence to do so. For example, the dog that uses the wind to locate the bird is exhibiting intelligence.

The dog must complete any assigned task. This task may be a retrieve over rough terrain or in cold and treacherous water. Courage displayed under these adverse conditions is a desirable trait. Labrador Retrievers have an innate desire to retrieve, but interest in and proper attitude toward the work are additional qualities that the retriever as a gundog should possess. These qualities are seen as alertness and eagerness during the retrieve. Judges refer to these qualities as

Trainers and Labrador Retriever enthusiasts travel across the country to attend and compete in field trials. Parking in isolated areas can mean a long walk to the test site.

"style." The retrieving dogs are rugged individuals and delight in such things as water retrieves in freezing weather. You should never endanger your dog; however, your dog must be willing to attempt to overcome all obstacles to complete the retrieve, no matter how insurmountable the obstacles may appear.

In addition to natural abilities, the Labrador Retriever must have "acquired abilities" in order to compete successfully. The first of these is general obedience. The obedient Labrador Retriever is always under control, whether he is close to you or far afield. Most trainers use a whistle, the type used by sports officials, to signal the dog when he is working at a distance. The basic obedience commands such as sit, stay, come, and heel are absolutely necessary in maintaining control of your dog and are certainly indispensable during competition. The Labrador Retriever must be trained not only to honor audible signals but also to honor visual signals, such as hand signals, and to respond positively to both.

An important attribute of the well-trained Labrador Retriever is his ability to complete blind retrieves. This means that

MHR and WR Sunnyview's Kachina, M.H., owned by Dick Weiner.

he responds to visual and audible direction signals that you give him to direct him to the area of the fall. The assumption is that the bird has fallen to the ground but the dog has not seen it. The Labrador Retriever is sent on a straight line toward the bird. The dog should not vary from this line, nor should he fail to negotiate any obstacle found in his path. He should proceed forward until you stop him. If the dog needs assistance in locating the bird, you provide hand signals to indicate direction. This continues until your dog finds the bird. Blind-retrieve training is considered advanced training, and only the mature Labrador Retriever should be asked to perform blind retrieves. However, proper early training includes exercises designed to encourage this ability. The retrieve is not complete until the bird has been delivered to the handler. The dog should return with purpose and speed, deliver the bird to hand, and give it up willingly. The bird should not be damaged by the dog; in fact, judges will penalize a Labrador Retriever for having a "hard mouth."

Choose the appropriate class for your dog and enter him properly. Licensed or member events are usually scheduled to last from two to five days. The majority of trials are scheduled for two to three days. This amount of time is necessary to complete all classes. If there has been adequate planning, the area for each test has been selected, and each test has been drawn up. Handlers, dogs, judges, and gallery gather at the area, and the trial is underway. First, a test dog is run. The purpose of this activity is to have a dog that is not entered in the trial attempt to complete the proposed test. If, as demonstrated by the test dog, the test is too difficult, it is altered. Having observed the test dog, handlers and judges feel confident that the test is fair and that it will be an accurate test of retrieving ability.

Entrants are then run in turn while the judges make careful observations and notes on each dog's performance. Another series is run, perhaps designed to test other abilities. This is designated the second series, and additional series are run until the judges are satisfied that they can make a definitive decision about each dog's abilities and performance for the day. Most judges are willing to discuss with you reasons for placing or scoring a particular dog or, on the other hand, why a particular dog was dropped from competition.

CHAMPIONSHIP STAKES

A discussion of the 2001 National Amateur Championship Stake may be beneficial to relate actual competitive situations and tests. The stake was run from June 17 to 23 in Virginia, Minnesota, in a region known as Iron Range country. Of the one hundred and ten retrievers entered there were ninety-seven black Labrador Retrievers, ten yellow, two chocolates, and one Golden Retrievers, but no Chesapeake Bay Retrievers. Ninety-one handlers were men and nineteen were women. Ten series were necessary to choose a winner, and it turned out to be

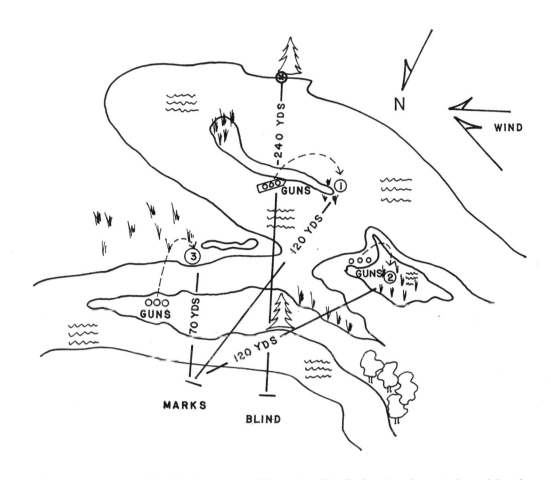

A map depicting a typical National Amateur Championship Stake. Numbers 1, 2, and 3 refer to a particular retrieves, and the X refers to the blind retrieve of the next series.

FC AFC Candlewood's Ramblin Man, a black male Labrador Retriever. Ram is owned by Dr. Judy and Jim Powers and was handled by Jim Powers.

The trial was run in an area with forests and lakes and is popular with campers, boaters and fishermen. It is a place with beautiful surroundings and with adequate area for multiple land and water retrieves. The trial grounds provided a variety of situations for the ten series. The tenth series was a difficult test that would only be completed by the very best retrievers. It was a land quadruple mark meaning that the dog had to remember the location of four birds!

The test was complicated by the fact that each mark required the dog to run across difficult terrain. The gallery had a great view of the test. The first bird down was a pheasant shot at about 250 yards.

The line to the bird was through heavy cattail cover initially and then through moderate cover. The second bird was a duck thrown about 125 yards from the line. It was difficult for the dog to navigate the thick cover to the bird. The third mark was a pheasant shot at about 185 yards and the final mark was a duck shot at 85 yards into a thick cattail swamp. The series was definitely set up to test the dog's marking ability and desire to retrieve.

Another example of a field-trial test for a finished Labrador Retriever is shown in the diagram above. It is an example of a water triple, which means that each dog must traverse water to each of the three falls. The test is somewhat complicated by the fact that several times the dog has to go from land to water and back to land to reach the bird. The line, or the position of the dog and handler, is on a steep slope

1995 NAFC and FC Ebonstar Lean Mac, owned by Sherwin Scott.

grass at point 3. The distance of this bird is approximately seventy yards from the line. This test is intended to determine the dog's marking ability. The difficulty of the test is the requirement that the dog remember marks while swimming through several channels of water for each of the three falls.

In addition to this test, another series could be set up in this same area where the dog would be required to do a blind retrieve in water. The blind retrieve is run across the same terrain as before, but the line is changed slightly. A dead duck is placed under a tree at point X, about 240 yards from the line. This test alone is very difficult, but to test the dog's ability to complete this blind retrieve without being diverted from his assigned task, gunners will shoot into the air and throw a dead duck. The Labrador Retriever should ignore this fallen duck and honor the signals and commands of the handler as he is directed to the blind.

From reading these brief descriptions of actual tests, you can better appreciate the actual abilities of the retrieving breeds and realize the complexity and difficulty of tests conceived to determine champions. The Labrador Retrievers successfully completing these tests have had expert training from individuals (both amateur and professional) who are totally dedicated to the sport. Each handler and trainer has made considerable effort to prepare the dog. Months of preparation and months and years of training for every conceivable retrieving situation require not only a well-bred and determined Labrador Retriever, but also an inspired and enthusiastic trainer. The reward for winning is more than a ribbon or trophy. The reward is the competition itself, and above all, the dog work. Not every Labrador Retriever will finish a championship. The frustrations and triumphs experienced in training become lifelong memories, which in the end are more valuable than championships.

overlooking the test area. From this vantage point the gunners can be seen.

Upon the judges' signal, the first fall is a dead duck thrown from a boat into the water at the end of an island, as shown at point 1 in the diagram. The gunners fire two shots. The second bird is a flighted mallard duck that will be shot to fall in shallow water with visible grass that is approximately 120 yards from the line at point 2. The third bird is a flighted pheasant that is shot to drop across a channel from the gunners into an area of native

TRAINING THE LABRADOR RETRIEVER FOR THE FIELD

A fter you acquire a Labrador Retriever puppy, you may decide to train him for hunting and perhaps for field trials or hunting tests. This decision may come as a result of your enjoyment of simply being around your dog or you may want to explore the extent of his abilities and enthusiasm. Or you may want to develop the natural retrieving instincts of the breed. Whatever your purpose for taking on the task of training for the field, the training regimen is the same. There are basic steps in training that the beginner *and* professional must follow in order to ensure success. Very early after you have made the decision, ask yourself the extent to which you want to train your dog. Will you just train for steadiness and single marks? Will you want your dog to complete double retrieves? Triple retrieves? What about blind retrieves? No matter what you decide, you must set goals and commit your time.

There have been great dogs that have done just about everything asked of them. Some were excellent hunting dogs that could have been competitive in field trials or hunting tests and other dogs that hunted when not on the field-trial or hunting-test circuit. One such dog was King Buck, a black male Labrador Retriever owned by John Olin of Winchester-Western fame. King Buck finished his ca-

reer with ninety-four championship points and won back-to-back National Championships, his second in 1957. King Buck also displayed his talents in the flooded timber of the Arkansas prairie retrieving wild ducks. The famous hunting clubs of the area, such as Greenbriar, north of Stuttgart, Arkansas, still exist. Dogs kenneled at Greenbriar and handled by Bill Benton and Chuck Myers carry on the tradition of King Buck, as do hunting and trial Labrador Retrievers from nearly every state in the Union.

All Labrador Retriever trainers agree that the breed is especially amenable to training. All that is required of you is a basic plan, common sense, and patience and respect for your dog. Your result will be an eager and faithful companion that will retrieve not only for the fun of it, but also to please you. Before you begin a training program, find resources that will give you information about training methods. Books and videos are great, but nothing beats talking with someone who has had dog-training experience. Seek out a person from a local retriever club and ask a lot of questions. Labrador Retriever people are happy to talk with you and help you solve your training problems. In the long run, you may even be a help to others.

Depending upon your dog's inherited abilities, you may want to vary the training

FC and AFC Discovery of Franklin, owned by John Olin.

program and at times even depart from conventional training methods. Regardless of your method, the most important aspects of successful training are *consistency* and *repetition*. Also to be considered is the fact that although training the retriever is not difficult, it does require a commitment of time. Once you begin your training schedule, you should not allow much to come between you and your training goals. *Critical training time is between six months and one year of age.* This chapter will help you work through this important time.

EARLY TRAINING

As soon as you bring your puppy home, introduce him to his new living quarters. This transition is important for a young puppy, and you need to make him as comfortable as possible. If the weather outside is harsh, confine him in the garage or other warm place. Weather permitting, place your dog in his perma-

nent quarters; for a field dog, this is preferably an outside kennel. Labrador Retrievers love cold weather, and it is not uncommon to see your Lab dozing in snow rather than a heated dog house.

Acclimation to a new home is itself a form of training and should be considered important as a means of developing early, sound training patterns. Early training is of paramount importance, because the approach used in training the young pup sets the stage for more regimented and difficult training at a later time. There are numerous habits that the young dog can develop early to enhance his trainability in the field. These habits will develop over his first six months of life.

Do not leave your puppy alone for long periods of time. He needs considerable attention from humans. This could take the form of a short stroll before each feeding. Allow your dog to be handled by people and exposed to human activities as much as possible. I know one breeder who hires people to come to his kennel just to play with and handle his puppies. That may be overkill, but you get the point. Strange sounds, especially abrupt noises, are simple curiosities to the puppy, and if he is properly introduced to different sounds at an early age, he will not become gunshy as an adult. Human voices, automobile sounds, and other noises provide valuable experiences for your puppy.

Experiences encountered by your puppy during short walks should also be considered early training. A walk in the field allows him time to explore. New scents and sights are experienced, and associations are made that lay the groundwork for future rigorous training sessions. Talk to your dog occasionally, using an affectionate expression such as "Good dog." The puppy will begin to recognize the tone of your voice and will respond in puppy fashion. This provides the basis for future training with voice commands. Finally, walks give your puppy a chance to get unrestricted exercise. Early training should also include a few minutes with your puppy during feeding time. Pet him and speak to him in a reassuring voice.

These routines may not appear at first glance to be important. However, one of the difficult tasks that you face in training is to have your dog respond in a positive way. The shy dog is almost impossible to train to retrieve. Therefore, early training is essentially grooming your puppy for future work. Your dog at some point in his development exhibits a sense of awareness for your actions. This is partially due to the Labrador Retriever's desire to please, and you need to be ready to take advantage of this innate quality.

Keep these early training sessions short. Your puppy will tire quickly and his interest will dissipate rapidly. A couple of ten- to fifteen-minute sessions per day is enough, but this time period may be expanded considerably as your dog matures. Brief training sessions in the beginning will ensure sharpness and interest at a later time. Make certain that early training sessions include exercises that are particularly pleasing to your puppy. End the training session and put your puppy back in the kennel while he is still alert. Anticipation for the next training session makes the puppy extremely eager, and this eagerness is perpetuated and seen in the mature dog.

One way to assure that your puppy retains his interest in you is to keep him in the kennel away from other dogs or people (even your wife/husband and children) prior to each training session. If you do this, you will be greeted warmly by a puppy that is anxious for attention and eager to participate in training activities. This is true not only for the puppy, but also for the mature dog.

SOME TRAINING RULES

Although other people mean to help, it is best to ask friends, spouses, and children *not* to attempt to train the puppy during your "serious" training except under your close supervision. Others may not understand your approach to training and may

Ch. West Wind Winchester, J.H., A.W.C., C.W.C., T.D.I., Can. C.D., owned by Nancy Brandow, Nick Mickelson, and Helen Ginnel.

actually hinder your progress. Others can work the dog later, because a finished Labrador Retriever will generally work for anyone. Even then, think twice before you lend your dog to anyone. A strange and perhaps awkward handler could confuse the dog and may harm his retrieving enthusiasm.

Occasionally, bad habits develop spontaneously and without obvious reason. Habits such as jumping up on people and barking in the kennel present problems. Deal with these behaviors as soon as they begin to develop. Decide which habits you wish to discourage. Generally, actions that make your dog a nuisance to other people are classified as bad habits. Most of your friends will praise your dog by telling you how impressive he is but will change their mind when he jumps up on them with muddy paws. Each bad habit presents a new challenge. Occasionally, you must be innovative in deciding upon a method that will break a bad habit. The method may be simple. For example, a raised knee intended to bump a jumping dog in the chest will discourage jumping. The command "no" or "down" should accompany the raised knee. You must be consistent and enforce the command each time your dog attempts to jump on someone.

An accepted method for punishing your dog is described in Chapter 6, but always use common sense. Use a stern "no" when necessary or "bad dog" spoken in a harsh and forceful tone. You may use these words even with a puppy that is eight weeks old. The dog's response is more to your tone of voice rather than to the word itself. Some trainers gently shake the dog while repeating the verbal reprimand and find this sufficient punishment. An association will quickly be made between the deed and the punishment, and the verbal command and its meaning will remain with your Lab his entire life. The same approach may be sufficient to stop your dog from barking, digging, or chewing.

The puppy enjoys time exploring his surrounding. Photo © Kent and Donna Dannen.

Occasionally, serious punishment must be given. It should, however, be given only to the extent necessary. Never punish your dog to the point where it constitutes physical abuse. Excessive physical punishment could cause your puppy to become shy and withdrawn. Do not allow your puppy to become constantly fearful of making a mistake that will be countered by punishment.

It is very important that you *administer a corrective punishment to a young dog at once*. In this way, the puppy associates the correction with the act. Punishment administered fifteen minutes after the fact only confuses the puppy. Make sure that there is no question about whether the puppy will understand why he is being reprimanded. With time, you will become familiar with the traits and habits of your dog, and it will become easier to determine the type and degree of punishment needed for him.

Be *consistent* in every act, especially with a young dog. Consistency is necessary if the dog is to develop an ability to respond positively to you. You also must develop patterns and be *repetitious* in training. Most professional trainers agree that dogs have little reasoning ability. Dogs do, however, develop a keen memory, which allows them to complete a task and do it with style if they have been asked to repeat this task over and over again. Therefore, retrieving perfection comes with repetition, which in turn develops memory. The secret to being a successful trainer is to be *consistent during training* and *repeat the tasks* you ask your dog to complete.

Too often you will give a command to the dog and not be in a position to enforce it. Each command must be enforced! The young dog knows when he can ignore a command. An embarrassing moment is when your dog ignores a command while other people are watching. On the other hand, you will be very proud when these same people see your dog respond immediately and with a positive attitude to a command. Consistency in enforcing a command teaches your

FC and AFC
Barracuda Blue,
owned by Charles
and Missy Tyson.

dog that the command is not a request but rather an ultimatum. The very first day you take your puppy for a training session, your influence should be felt. This influence might appear to others to be nothing but intimidation, but it does not matter what you call it as long as you have *control* of your dog. A well-trained dog will always feel that he is under the control of his trainer, and, consequently, he will always anticipate some command. If the dog has been influenced in this way, he is quick to respond and appears to be eager and willing to complete a task.

Experience with Labrador Retrievers has shown that they not only respond to this attitude, but also thrive on such a relationship with their trainer. Most dog owners allow their pets to wander aimlessly about, no matter where they are. This simply does not command a dog's attention. As an example, if your dog is under control, you can easily call him to your side if a strange dog enters the yard. Control could also be defined as the atti-

tude of your dog when he is obeying a command. Nothing will deter him from his assigned task. In brief, control is the frame of mind of your dog as he anticipates and obeys a command.

ENVIRONMENTAL CONDITIONING

There are two important qualities that the older dog must have to be a good retriever. The first is having no aversion to gunshot, and the second is having a love for water. Both of these qualities can and should be instilled in the young puppy during early training. It has been mentioned that the puppy should be exposed to common, everyday noise as well as to other abrupt noises. Any noise that is unusual, with the exception of exploding fireworks, is a helpful training aid.

At some point, however, you must introduce your puppy to the gun. This is best done using a small-caliber firearm. Safely

American and Canadian Ch. Minnesota Mike II, owned by Kenneth Bliss, shows the eagerness with which a Labrador Retriever can enter the water.

FC Mick the Quick, owned by M. McGee is alert to things around him.

shoot into the air or ground when your puppy is at a distance and is least expecting it. Chances are the pup will run to you. Praise and reassure him. Be very careful not to frighten him. Otherwise, you may do irreparable damage at this point in training. Continue the routine until you can fire the gun with the pup next to you without unduly startling him. With this accomplished, repeat the same lesson with a shotgun. Never shoot any gun so that your dog's ears are hurt by the muzzle blast. You can avoid this by positioning the dog behind the gun. In time, a gunshot will be the signal to retrieve.

The Labrador Retriever has an inherent love for the water, but this must be nurtured. You must water-train your puppy so that he will accept water and water retrieves enthusiastically as a mature dog. The two-month-old puppy will accept water if he is properly introduced to it. A walk along the edge of a lake or stream is the type of exposure that the puppy needs. He will find water interesting and exciting and before long will be taking swims without your prompting him. Winter months are not the best for introducing your puppy to water, but retrieves from cold water should be required of the mature dog. Another dog in the water is helpful in persuading the puppy to enter water. If another dog is not available, be willing to wade in yourself. Clap your hands and speak in an excited voice to coax your puppy into the water. Never throw your dog into the water with the intent of teaching him to swim. Once a good association with water has been made, the dog will enter again without hesitation. After he is introduced to water, your dog's enthusiasm for water will be maintained by frequent trips to the lake, marsh, pond, or stream.

TRAINING EQUIPMENT

Before you begin serious training, purchase several training aids. The first is a metal, chain-link collar. The collar should fit just over your dog's head and hang loosely around his neck. Also buy a short leather leash with a snap at one end. Most trainers use a whistle to command their dog when he is working at a distance. Choose the type used by sports officials, and put it on a lanyard that can be hung around your neck. Finally, buy a dozen or more training dummies. The dummy, or bumper, is used in training as a substitute for ducks, pheasants, or other game birds. Dummies are usually cylindrical in shape and are constructed of either plasticized rubber or cork covered with heavy canvas. Start your puppy with a small dummy, perhaps one that is homemade, and use larger ones for the mature dog. Most of these items can be purchased from a pet store or ordered from a hunting-dog specialty store. Another popular training aid, a device for propelling training dummies, uses blank cartridges as the propellant. It will throw dummies to distances beyond those possible otherwise.

Available also, but recommended only for the professional trainer, is an electric collar. With it you can administer a mild electric shock as a means of training. If you are a novice trainer and plan to use the electric collar for training, understand its use fully, or your dog may react negatively. The electric shock will not harm the dog, but it *will* make a lasting impression.

Each individual has different ideas about the age at which a pup becomes trainable and the age at which a serious attempt should be made to train for obedience and retrieving. The perfect time depends upon a variety of factors. You will see dogs less than one year of age competing in field trials and hunting tests, but this is rare. Table 10-1 shows the approximate age at which to start the various aspects of obedience training.

FC and AFC Esprit Playin' For Keeps, owned by Mitchel P. Brown.

The novice trainer is usually impatient and finds it difficult to wait until the dog reaches a trainable age. There is no magical age, but the dog should be at least six months old before beginning training and at least eight months old before starting serious training. Rigorous training of the young dog tends to cause the dog to lose enthusiasm and interest. The dog becomes stale and may even hesitate to obey. During the first six months of the puppy's life, you need only establish a routine that includes simple discipline. Each exercise attempted before six months of age should be pleasant for the dog. The six-month-old dog is mentally developed to handle strict obedience commands, and the

TABLE 10-1. A SUGGESTED SCHEDULE FOR OBEDIENCE TRAINING DURING THE FIRST YEAR.

ACTIVITY	AGE OF DOG
Playtime, humanization, the command NO! and "good dog"	6 weeks to 6 months
Serious obedience training	6 months to 8 months
Frequent reinforcement of all commands	8 months to 12 months

TABLE 10-2. THE MANY FACTORS INVOLVED IN PRODUCING THE OBEDIENT DOG.

Common sense training   Repetition of drills

Duplication of training techniques   Positive training sessions

Obedient Dog   Praise for success

Tolerance of mistakes

Health maintenance

Introduction to different environments   Discipline for trainer

eight-month-old dog is physically developed to handle retrieving. As the dog continues to mature, more and more may be asked of him. Factors involved in training for obedience are shown in Table 10-2.

FORMAL TRAINING

The first lessons in formal training should be the obedience commands. All Labrador Retrievers should be taught the simple commands to heel, sit (stay), and come, whether or not they will ever be expected to retrieve. (Some use sit to mean just sit, but others use sit to mean sit and stay.) All of these commands are explained in Table 10-3. An obedient dog is not a nuisance to family or friends. Obedience for the retrieving dog is absolutely necessary, and this training should precede formal retrieving training (see Chapter 6, "Manners for Your Labrador Retriever").

A trainable dog will be responding to obedience commands within four to six months. It is good practice to preface each command with your dog's name so that when his name is spoken, he anticipates a command. For example, try: "Brandy, Sit!" Or, "Brandy, Come!" Pause briefly after giving the dog's name. This will cause your dog to anticipate the command that is to follow. While teaching obedience commands, familiarize your dog with the whistle. After giving the

verbal command "Sit," follow immediately with one sharp blast on the whistle. Either the word "sit" or one blast on the whistle should mean to sit. When your dog is near you, you may use the verbal command, but when he is at a distance, you may find it necessary to use the whistle. The whistle will carry farther than your voice. The dog should respond quickly to either the voice or whistle command. The whistle is also useful in calling your dog to you. After giving the verbal command "Come," immediately follow with two or more blasts on the whistle. Your dog will learn to come to either the verbal command or the whistle command.

Once you have started formal training, it is not unusual for your dog to become confused and not understand what you are attempting to do. It is very important during these times to think through your situation and alter your training to overcome your dog's confusion. Perhaps the best advice applicable to all training situations is that you always use common sense. When your dog is confused, analyze the situation and determine the reason for the confusion. For example, never command your dog to come to be punished. He will be confused because he will associate the punishment with the fact that he obeyed the command "Come." What do you think he will do the next time you call him? A common-sense analysis of the problem would indicate

TABLE 10-3. FREQUENTLY USED OBEDIENCE COMMANDS.

Command	Use	Comment
No	Used anytime to prevent or stop an undesirable action	Used to stop barking, whining, jumping, etc.
Good dog	A command used frequently to praise your dog	Useful to indicate your pleasure for a particular action
Heel	a. Given for the dog to assume a sitting position facing forward on the left side of the trainer b. Walk with the trainer on his/her left side and the pace may vary	a. Used primarily to position the dog for further commands b. Helpful to move the dog "under control" from one position to another
Sit	a. Sit anywhere, anytime the command is spoken b. May be used instead of "stay" to command the dog to remain in one place	a. Useful when you want the dog to stop other things and anticipate further commands b. Used anytime you want your dog to stay while you move about
Come	This commands the dog to immediately come to you and sit at your left side	Used frequently, especially when you want your dog near you

that you should go to your dog to administer punishment.

I was once invited on a duck hunt with a young trainer eager to show me the results of his retriever training ability. He had trained a well-bred, yellow female Labrador Retriever. We hunted from a shore blind on a large reservoir with decoys spread in shallow water in front of the blind. The dog sat patiently watching the sun come up on a cool November morning and was obviously anxious to retrieve. I was impressed by her steadiness and eagerness to go to work.

Shortly, a flock of ringneck ducks buzzed the decoys, and when my young trainer friend said "Take 'em," I scratched one down just outside the decoys. The dog was steady as a rock, and upon her master's command, enthusiastically jumped into the water. As she swam through the decoys, she suddenly swung sharply to the right, far from the floating duck, and grabbed a decoy, which she promptly began dragging back to the blind as proud as could be. Her trainer was livid! He jumped up and down and yelled, "No! No! No!" I felt sorry for both handler and dog at that point. When she finally

got to the bank, he punished her severely and promptly apologized to me for having forced me to watch such a stupid dog.

The remainder of the morning passed slowly; no more ducks were to be seen. When we were ready to go home, I indicated that I would put on waders and help pick up decoys. My young hunter friend said, "No, my dog will do it! Watch, this is a neat trick." With that, he picked up a large rock and threw it so that it made a large splash in the middle of the decoy spread. He then lined his dog and sent her into the decoys with the intention of having her drag the decoys to the bank. She refused to go into the water. Once again, I was witness to a wild man jumping and screaming at his dog, because this time she would not retrieve a decoy. "Wait a minute," I said. "Earlier this morning you punished her for bringing in a decoy, and now you expect her to do what you just taught her not to do. She is totally confused!" With that, he realized what he was doing wrong. On the drive back home we talked about the importance of thinking through all training and hunting situations and the value of using *common sense* in training.

NFC and AFC San Joaquin Honcho, owned by J. Aycock.

Many times, a novice trainer will allow his or her dog to refuse to follow commands. This is very bad practice, and the dog quickly realizes that he may or may not have to obey. Enforce every command and make certain that your dog responds with immediate and positive action to each command. If you insist on sharp obedience, the dog will maintain this attitude while retrieving.

In addition to the basic obedience commands, other commands are useful that should be taught early. The first is "Kennel." This command may be used not only to instruct your dog to enter the kennel, but also to instruct him to enter the car or truck, front or back door, or any other appropriate place. To teach this command, first give your dog the command to sit. Then command "Kennel," and coax your dog into the kennel. Repeat the command several times so that the association is made between entering the kennel and the command. Many trainers make an exaggerated gesture with their hand toward the open kennel. This gesture is helpful later when commanding your dog to enter something that is unfamiliar. It shows your dog exactly what is expected.

Another useful command is the release command. There should be times when your dog is allowed to run and exercise without feeling restricted. Let him run only where it is safe, and where people will not be apprehensive about a free-running dog. Various terms such as "Okay" or "All right" may be used to release your dog. "Okay" is commonly used. The best way to teach this command is to use the word often during short walks with your puppy. He occasionally will come to you, and as he turns to run to play, give the command. The pup will associate the release command with leaving your side. Use the release command any time when you do not want your dog at heel. Each time your dog performs a command properly, be sure to praise him and remember to repeat the commands over and over again each practice session.

Once your retriever has mastered the first few lessons, you will find that he will learn additional lessons more quickly. The reason is that your dog has become aware of what is expected and, therefore, is more likely to respond positively to additional training. More importantly, your dog will begin to use prior training and associations to complete new assignments. This could be called the "snowball effect," and you should use it to advantage. You will realize this effect, however, only if you thoroughly master each step in training before you go on to the next step. Even then, early lessons must be repeated frequently.

RETRIEVER TRAINING SESSIONS

It is imperative that you spend early training sessions alone with your puppy. Other people, dogs, noises, and minor interruptions are distractions that break the pup's concentration. Find a quiet area of the backyard or maybe even use the garage as your training area. When your pup is doing well with obedience, move to other places. Choose areas where there are minor distractions, but enforce the commands absolutely. Local kennel clubs hold practice sessions for the purpose of acclimating puppies to minor distractions. Check out the parks and golf courses in your area after you are familiar with local leash laws. Parks make excellent training areas.

Later, as your dog begins retrieving, it will become more important to find unique training areas. Check for areas that provide a variety of terrain. Duck marshes, wildlife areas, farm ponds, streams, and rivers are all potential training sites. As you make frequent trips to these areas to familiarize your pup with varied surroundings, your dog's anticipation for the job at hand will heighten. It is advantageous to make friends with farmers who have large ponds or lakes that may be used for future water training. Be sure to select some training areas where you will be allowed to shoot a gun.

When you start your pup on retrieving, make sure that the object thrown is a training dummy made especially for this purpose. Never throw a stick, a beer can, or other novel item and expect your dog to retrieve it. As training progresses, occasionally substitute birds for the training dummies.

The easiest way to interest your pup in the object is to tease him with it. Drag the dummy along the ground and swing it into the air, all the time speaking to the pup in an excited voice. Use the word "bird" frequently. Curiosity will cause your pup to attempt to take the dummy. At the height of your pup's excitement, pitch the dummy so that it will fall in full view. Instinctively, he will run to pick it up. As soon as he has the dummy in his mouth, begin to run backward, clapping your hands to encourage him to follow. Take advantage of the fact that the puppy is running to you and blow the "come" command on the whistle. This deed reinforces a command learned earlier. The pup will catch up, and when he does, reach

To train the dog's mouth for retrieving he is first taught to hold the dummy.

The transition from dummy to live duck is an easy one for a well-conditioned dog. This live duck was used over and over for an entire training season.

At the conclusion of the retrieve the dog should deliver to hand.

down and take the dummy from him. Your dog will have completed his first retrieve. Repeat this over and over again at each training session. Some professionals use this even with the mature dog to heighten enthusiasm or as a break from normal training.

It is imperative that good retrieving patterns be established at this point. Just as with all other aspects of training, retrieving the dummy must be completed properly. When tempting the pup with the dummy, do not allow him to drag it and tug at it. This makes him reluctant to release the bird properly during later training and encourages "hard mouth." Do not allow your pup to play with the dummy instead of returning it. If your pup refuses to return with the dummy, you must be more expressive in encouraging him. Try running around a corner of the house to arouse his curiosity. He will run to investigate. Take the dummy from him as soon as possible, preferably before he drops it.

Your dog will soon associate your taking the dummy with the act of retrieving. This simple exercise will discourage dropping a bird later and will make training to "deliver to hand" easier.

Once you have begun retrieving, continue it. Three or four retrieves each training session are sufficient in the beginning. A few retrieves will not bore the pup, and the time to return the pup to the kennel is when he shows the first signs of tiring. Do not force a young puppy to continue an exercise when you are making no progress. It is best to put the pup away and start fresh the next day. This will assure that he will be anxious to begin again. An important training fundamental is maintaining enthusiasm.

RETRIEVING THE BIRD

Some trainers want their dog to drop the bird at their feet when completing a retrieve. The preferred method, however, is to have the dog hold the bird until it is taken from him. All field-trial and hunting-test trainers (and most hunters) require their dogs to deliver to hand. This means that the dog must return with the bird, sit at heel with the bird in his mouth, and hold it until the handler takes it. The commands "Leave it," "Release," or "Give" are frequently used here. Teaching to deliver to hand is a rather difficult and critical phase of training. Before you attempt to have your dog "hold" the bird, he should be showing a great deal of enthusiasm for retrieving and should feel comfortable with the bird in his mouth.

This phase of training should be conducted in the basement or garage, clearly removed from other training areas. You do not want your dog to make any bad associations between being forced to hold the bird and retrieving in the field. The purpose of these training sessions is to force your dog to hold the dummy (and later the bird) until you take it from him. To begin, pry your dog's mouth open with gentle pressure and force the dummy in while repeating the command "Fetch" or "Hold." Praise your dog! Hold his mouth closed for a few seconds, then slowly release it. Chances are, your dog will drop the dummy. Quickly force it back into his mouth, repeating "Fetch." After he has held the dummy for a few seconds, take it from him while you repeat the command "Give." Repeat this lesson daily until your dog will take the dummy from you and release it upon command.

Once your dog has thoroughly mastered this lesson, combine it with retrieving. Have your dog sit at heel and hold the dummy for extended periods of time. Give the command to stay, and walk a few steps away. Stop, and give the command to "come" and "heel". If at any time your dog drops the dummy, quickly force it back into his mouth while repeating "Fetch." The next step is to throw the dummy and, as your dog returns with it, give the command to heel. If he attempts to drop the dummy, quickly give the command to fetch. With your dog at heel, speak the command "Give" and take the dummy. When the retrieve is complete, praise your dog! Once you have completed the task of training your dog to deliver to hand, incorporate it into all phases of retrieving .

TRAINING AREAS

Once your pup has become accustomed to retrieving from land areas, take him to water. Assuming that he has been properly introduced to water as a puppy, retrieving from water should present no real difficulties. Use the same technique to excite the pup. Throw the dummy so that it falls into the water just a few feet from the bank. If your puppy was reluctant to enter water previously, water retrieves of this nature may stimulate his interest. The first few sessions should be conducted in shallow water and then gradually changed to deep water or to water with obstacles, such as lily pads and stumps.

When your dog has mastered the single "sight" retrieve on land, begin to throw

The well-trained Labrador Retriever is eager to please. Training methods are devised to take advantage of this inherent characteristic of the breed.

the dummy so that it lies where it is not in clear view of your dog. Short grass works well. This will be a new challenge for your pup, and chances are he will be confused at not being able to see the dummy. Instinct should overcome his confusion, however, and he should begin "hunting."

A common mistake made by most puppies is to begin hunting before reaching the area of the fall. Make the first retrieves *short* in order to avoid this problem, and extend them as training progresses. Before he gives up, encourage the pup by running to the fall and excitedly repeating, "Dead bird." Praise him when he finds it! The command "Dead bird" or other appropriate command will be helpful in the field later when your dog is looking for a lost bird. As your dog becomes more proficient at finding the bird, do not be too quick to help. Allow him to hunt, and actually encourage it.

Advanced training requires the help of others. You may also want assistance in planning the training session to get the maximum benefit for your dog.

He should hunt the general area of the fall, however, and not leave the area to hunt elsewhere. Insist that the retrieve be completed, and remember to enforce this rule at all times.

Every Labrador Retriever will eventually make a mistake and "get into trouble." Accept this fact of life and be very patient when it happens. Even field champions make mistakes. If possible, avoid letting your dog make the mistake in the first place. Your dog must be shown that a mistake has been made, and corrective action must be taken if necessary. Many of these situations can be avoided by planning your training sessions carefully so that your dog is not asked to negotiate a retrieve that is beyond his capabilities or stage of training.

Chances are your dog will realize the importance of his nose while retrieving dummies from cover. Even though a scent has not been applied to the dummy, there is sufficient scent associated with it that it can be smelled easily by the dog, especially downwind. Some trainers prefer to scent the dummy lightly with anise oil.

The pup will develop an ability to use his nose without further help from you.

Ask your retriever to make more and more difficult retrieves as his abilities improve. Increase the distance both on land and in water. Always make certain that your dog has a clear view of the falling bird and that he can negotiate the terrain. Some examples of obstacles that your dog should be asked to negotiate are ditches, creeks, and plowed fields. Begin to teach the "mark" command, which is commonly used to alert your dog to watch for a bird to fall. The command "Mark" is given just prior to throwing the dummy.

TRAINING ASSISTANCE

Eventually, you will need help in training. The person asked to help must be an individual who is especially anxious to see the dog trained well and one who will be patient with you and with your dog. The most important task for the helper is to serve as the "bird thrower." The only requisites for this person are that he or she has a good throwing arm and be able to throw the bird in a wide arc to a predetermined area. The bird thrower should either fire a gun or yell (for example, yell "Hey" three or four times) to attract the dog's attention, throw the bird, then remain quiet and motionless until the dog has completed the retrieve. The bird thrower is an important individual and is indispensable to the trainer.

STEADYING YOUR DOG

Up to this point, you have simply thrown the dummy and your dog has more or less chased it. Eventually, it becomes necessary to "steady" your dog. This term means that your dog is trained to sit patiently at your side while the dummy is thrown. He must be trained not to go to the fall (dummy or bird) until you send him. The phrase "steady to shot" means the same thing, but this training should not be attempted until your dog is retrieving enthusiastically. You are asking your dog to exercise patience, which is difficult, especially for an excitable and high-spirited pup.

Before you begin this phase, decide upon a command to use to send your dog to the fallen bird. Many people use the dog's name, while others use the word "back." The check or slip-cord method may be used to steady your dog when you begin this phase of training. Tie a small-diameter rope about four feet long to the left side of your belt, pass the other end through your dog's collar, then hold it behind you with your right hand. Command your dog to sit at heel. To alert your dog, use the command "Mark." Then have the bird thrower throw the dummy. Repeat the command "Sit" or "Stay" while you hold the check cord tightly. Chances are your dog will tug and spin in an attempt to go to the fall. Immediately, speak the command "Back," and release the cord from your right hand. As your dog runs, the free end of the cord will slide through his collar and he will be free to complete

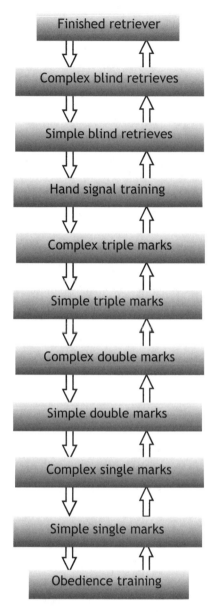

The ladder method for training the retriever. Each rung prepares the handler for the next step. As you progress up the ladder, you should frequently step back down to reinforce earlier concepts and you may stop at any level you wish.

the retrieve. Repeat this often, each time extending the time before you release your dog. Eventually, require your dog to stay for any period of time until you send him. A totally steady dog should be able to sit and watch without breaking even while another dog retrieves. Use the slip cord for a long period of time even after your dog is steady to prevent his developing the habit of "breaking."

1. Dr. Richard L. Myers, co-author, demonstrates the slip-cord method of steadying the dog. The cord is attached to the handler's belt.

2. The cord is passed through the dog's collar.

3. The cord is first held in the handler's left hand behind the dog's head.

4. The cord is then transferred to the handler's right hand and held behind the back to free the handler's left hand.

MULTIPLE MARKS

Eventually, you will want to advance to training for multiple marks. The idea is to simulate a hunting situation where two or three ducks have been shot out of a flock and are on the water. Your dog will have been trained to "mark these down" and will methodically retrieve each one, one at a time. To move from one plan to the other, progress from the simple to the more complex as shown in the figure explaining the ladder concept. You always can move back down the ladder (see illustration on page 87) to reinforce skills taught earlier. Likewise, you may skip rungs on the ladder on the way back down and are encouraged to do so. The dog that is learning triple marks should occasionally get a fun single mark or two as well.

As soon as your Labrador Retriever is steady, start him on double marks. Here he will be asked to watch and to mark two birds thrown in succession. Most dogs will first retrieve the last bird thrown. Require your dog to complete this retrieve properly before you send him for the next bird. Your dog should heel and sit, release the bird, and go for the next bird only upon command. Likewise, teach him to retrieve triple marks. Begin with simple doubles and triples, then proceed to more complicated retrieves.

BLIND RETRIEVES

Another advanced phase is training for blind retrieves. A "blind" is a retrieve of a bird that falls to the ground or water but is not seen by the dog. You, however, know the exact location and are able to direct your retriever to the bird with a series of whistle and hand signals. This retrieve is required in some field-trial and hunting-test stakes and is useful in many hunting situations. Training for this retrieve requires that your dog be well schooled in other phases of retrieving. The point at which blind-retrieve training begins varies but depends primarily on your dog's progress with other phases of his training.

The initial step is an exercise in retrieving "sight blinds." Take your dog to an area such as a golf course, where the grass will not conceal the training dummy. Tell your dog to stay, then walk away about twenty-five yards, drop the dummy, and return to your dog. This distance will be increased later, because eventually you can expect your dog to complete retrieves up to 150 yards or more. The dog should see you drop the dummy. This is a new aspect of training, and your Lab may be temporarily confused because he has seen no one throw the dummy, and he has not "marked the fall." Nevertheless, you should expect him to make the transition from retrieving "marks" to completing blind retrieves.

With your dog at heel, extend your left hand, palm open, above your dog's head in an obvious pointing gesture toward the dummy. A command that is commonly used to alert the dog to the expected retrieve is "Line." Then use the verbal command to retrieve ("Back" or your dog's name). Because the dummy is in full view of your dog, he should bound out and retrieve it enthusiastically. Keep the exercise simple in the beginning, and do not force your dog to do long or complicated retrieves. Repeat this exercise often so that your dog will learn quickly that "Line" and a hand direction mean that there is a bird somewhere along the imaginary line laid out by your gesture. Do not hide the dummy, because this will cause your dog to begin to "hunt" rather than to trust you for proper direction. Hunting on a blind retrieve is an undesirable habit. You need to have total control of your dog and must be able to override his hunting instinct. Your dog's use of his nose, however, is indispensable in the blind retrieve.

To aid him in finding the bird, teach your dog hand signals that indicate left, right, back, or in. More advanced dogs are taught angle directions. Hand-signal training may be taught concurrently with sight blinds.

Once again, the golf course can be used. Set up an imaginary baseball diamond with

The proper way to give direction or "line" to a blind retrieve.

The dog moves to the left in response to the handler's signal during a blind retrieve.

The dog moves to the right in response to the handler's signal during a blind retrieve.

The Labrador Retriever anticipates the "back" command during a blind retrieve.

first, second, third, and home bases. Have your dog sit on the pitcher's mound, give the command "Sit (Stay)," and walk over and drop a dummy on first base. Allow your dog to see this and make certain that the dummy is in full view. Walk to home plate and stand facing your dog. Extend your right arm horizontally and indicate the direction to the dummy. Simultaneously shout the command "Over." Your dog should run to the dummy, pick it up, and bring it in. You may have to encourage your dog at first, but in a short time he will master this exercise.

Next, teach "Over" to third base. Periodically repeat the retrieve from first base. Teach "Back" using the same technique. Place the bumper at second base. With your dog on the pitcher's mound, signal from home base with a raised arm and give the command "Back." Likewise, place the bumper in front of your dog and signal with a downward sweep of your arm and a trill on the whistle. Practice these exercises in water so that your dog learns to handle in water as well as on land. Remember to repeat these drills at each training session until your dog is able to complete each command with precision.

Only after these drills have been mastered should you take your Lab to training areas where you can place the dummy in cover. Repeat the training techniques that you used on the golf course to allow your dog to make the transition from retrieving the bird that is in full view to retrieving a bird from cover. After this is accomplished, you may attempt the actual blind retrieve where you bring sight-blind training and hand-signal training together.

Start by placing the dummy in an area that presents no major obstacles. Do not try to hide the dummy. Simply place it in a spot so that the dummy is not visible to your dog from the line or from the starting point. Keep in mind that the retrieve should be completed with as little difficulty as possible, and that if your dog takes a good initial line to the bird, he will be in a better position for hand signals. The dog that has been well schooled on

sight blinds will take a good line, and the dog that has mastered hand signals can be easily directed to the bird.

The blind retrieve is accomplished by having your dog at heel. Give the direction and the appropriate verbal command. Your dog should charge out and continue on the imaginary line directly to the bird. Chances are, however, your dog will vary direction from that line because of some obstacle, such as a ditch, and direction must be corrected. Stop your dog with one short blast on the whistle. You earlier taught your dog to sit on the whistle during obedience training. Remember? Then give one of the four hand signals with a verbal command. A series of commands may be necessary to work your dog to the blind. Eventually, he will find the bird and proudly deliver it to you.

Always devise a training test that you know can be completed by your dog. Success during a training session is important to your dog's continued development.

Ch. Star's Sailerman of Seasac C.D.X., W.C., owned by Art and Beth Davis.

THE FINISHED
LABRADOR RETRIEVER

Many professionals have proven that the techniques described here work and that the dog makes a smooth transition from training sessions to field trials, hunting tests, or hunting in the field. There are things that you should do during training, however, to ensure that your dog makes the transition with a minimum of difficulty. For example, include duck decoys in training sessions. Introduction of decoys can be done on land first by simply walking your dog through decoys scattered around the backyard. Throw a dummy among the decoys and have your dog retrieve the dummy without picking up a decoy. Scold him if he attempts to retrieve a decoy. Then put the decoys in water and command your dog to retrieve through them.

Introduce your dog to real birds gradually. One trick is to tape a duck or pheasant wing to a training dummy and tease your dog with it. The scent will arouse his interest. Suddenly pitch the dummy and allow your dog to run to it and pick it up. Make him bring it to you. Try the same thing with a dead or shackled duck. Take the bird from the dog immediately. Do not allow him to play with anything that you have commanded him to retrieve. Obviously, ducks and pheasants are not easy to get for training, but pigeons are a good substitute and can be bought locally at reasonable prices for use in training.

At your discretion, take your Labrador Retriever to an actual field trial or hunting test, or on a hunting trip. This is a very important day. All of the principles used in training should apply in these situations. If your dog has been trained properly, no problem should arise, but if one does, approach it just as if it were another problem encountered in training. Force your dog to realize that even though these events are more fun than a training session, the same rules apply, and the ultimate task is to retrieve the fallen game.

The experiences encountered in the field and shared by you and your dog are lasting and are unequaled by any other experiences. They will make you a better trainer. But also remember to seek additional help from other sources. You will be able to find books that deal with specific aspects of advanced training, such as blind retrieves, and you will see videos that provide specifics about water work. Choose your resources carefully and make certain that the techniques described fit into your overall goals and expectations for your Labrador Retriever.

SHOW COMPETITION FOR THE LABRADOR RETRIEVER

Centuries ago it was common practice to hold agricultural fairs in conjunction with spring and fall religious festivals, and to these gatherings, cattle, dogs, and other livestock were brought for exchange. As time went on, it also became customary to provide entertainment. Dogs often participated in sporting events such as bull baiting, bear baiting, and ratting. The dog that exhibited the greatest skill in the arena was also the one that brought the highest price when time came for barter or sale. Today these fairs seem a far cry from our highly organized bench shows, field trials, and hunting tests. They were, however, the forerunners of modern dog shows and played an important role in shaping the development of purebred dogs.

The first organized dog show was held at Newcastle, England, in 1859. Later that same year, a show was held at Birmingham. At both shows, dogs were divided into four classes and only pointers and setters were entered. In 1860, the first dog show in Germany was held at Apoldo. Nearly 100 dogs were exhibited, and entries were divided into six groups. Interest expanded rapidly, and by the time the Paris Exhibition was held in 1878, the dog show was a fixture of international importance.

In the United States, the first organized bench show was held in 1874 in conjunction with the meeting of the Illinois State Sportsmen's Association in Chicago, and all entries were dogs of the sporting breeds. Although the show was a rather casual affair, interest spread quickly. Before the end of the year, shows had been held in Oswego, New York, Mineola, Long Island, and Memphis, Tennessee. The latter combined a bench show with the first organized field trial ever held in the United States. In January 1875, an all-breed show, the first in the United States, was held in Detroit, Michigan. From that point on, interest increased rapidly. Rules were not always uniform, however, because there was no organization through which to coordinate activities until September 1884, when the American Kennel Club was founded. Now the largest dog-registering organization in the world, the AKC is an association of more than 500 member clubs. These clubs represent all-breed, specialty, performance, and obedience groups, and each is represented by a delegate to the AKC.

There are approximately 15,541 shows and events held annually in the United States, and these functions do much to stimulate interest in breeding to produce better-looking, sounder, purebred dogs. For breeders, shows provide a means of measuring the merits of their work as compared with accomplishments of other

Ch. Highlands Space Ranger was the No. 1 Labrador Retriever Breed System, 1995. Owned by G. Knobloch. © JC Photo.

breeders. For hundreds of thousands of dog fanciers, they provide an absorbing hobby.

CONFORMATION SHOWS

At bench shows, which are also called conformation shows, dogs are rated comparatively on their physical qualities, or how well they conform to the Breed Standard that has been approved by the AKC. Characteristics such as size, coat, color, placement of the eye or ear, and general soundness are the basis for selecting the best dog in a class. Only purebred dogs are eligible to compete, and if the show awards points toward a championship, a dog must be at least six months of age.

Bench shows are of various types. An all-breed show has classes for all of the breeds recognized by the AKC, as well as a Miscellaneous Class for breeds not yet recognized. A sanctioned match is an informal meeting where dogs compete, but not for championship points. A specialty show is confined to a single breed. Other shows may restrict entries to champions

of record, to Bred-by-Exhibitor dogs, or others. Competition for Junior Showmanship or Best Brace, Best Team, or Best Local Dog may be included. Obedience competition is frequently held in conjunction with bench shows.

The term "bench show" is somewhat confusing in that shows of this type may either be "benched" or "unbenched." At the former, each dog is assigned an individually numbered stall, where he must remain throughout the show except for times when he is being judged, groomed, or exercised. At unbenched shows, no stalls are provided, and dogs are kept in their owners' cars or in crates when not being judged.

The Classes

A show in which a dog is judged for conformation actually constitutes an elimination contest. To begin with, the dogs of a single breed compete with others of their breed in one of the regular classes: Puppy, Bred by Exhibitor, American-Bred, or Open, and finally, Winners, where the top dogs of the preceding classes meet. The next step is the judging for Best of

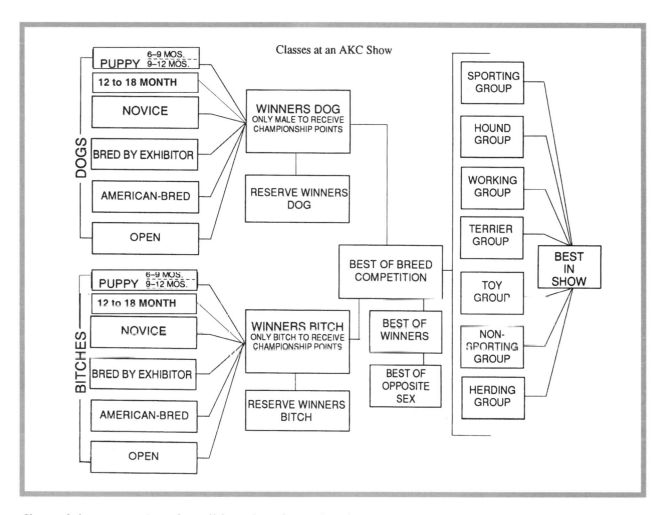

Chart of the progression of an all-breed conformation show.

Breed or Best of Variety if a breed has more than one variety. Here the Winners Dog and the Winners Bitch compete with any champions that are entered, together with any undefeated dogs that have competed in an additional nonregular class. The dog named Best of Breed then goes on to compete with the other Best-of-Breed winners in his Group. The dogs that win in Group competition then compete for the final and highest honor, Best in Show.

The winners of the Winners Dog and the Winners Bitch class are awarded championship points. The number of points awarded varies depending upon factors such as the number of dogs competing, the Schedule of Points established by the Board of Directors of the AKC for each geographical region of the country, and whether the dog goes Best of Win-

ners, Best of Breed, Group I, or Best in Show.

In order to become a champion, a dog must win fifteen points, including points from at least two major wins—that is, at least two shows where three or more points are awarded. The major wins must be under two different judges, and one or more of the remaining points must be won under a third judge. The most points ever awarded at a show is five and the least is one. In order to become a champion, a dog must therefore be exhibited and must win in at least three shows. Usually he is shown many times before he wins his championship.

The *AKC Gazette* and other dog magazines print lists of forthcoming shows, together with the names and addresses of sponsoring organizations to which you

Specialty shows are limited to one breed and are held by regional and national breed specific clubs such as the Labrador Retriever Club of America. Specialty shows often include "non-regular" classes such as brace, stud dog and brood bitch, or veterans.
Left: Ch. Ridgeview Heartland Hitman owned by Kevin and Sandy McCabe.
Right: Two Could Be's Labs, owned by Barbara Hogan, win a Brace Class. Petrulis Photo.

may write for entry forms and information relative to fees, closing dates, and location. Before you enter your dog for the first time in a show, familiarize yourself with the regulations and rules governing competition. This information may be secured from the AKC or from a local dog club that specializes in a particular breed. It is essential that you learn about the AKC-approved Standard for the Breed so that you will be fully aware of characteristics worthy of merit as well as those considered faulty, or possibly even serious enough to disqualify your dog from competition. For instance, monorchidism and cryptorchidism are disqualifying faults in all breeds.

If possible, first attend a show as a spectator and observe judging procedures from ringside. It will also be helpful to join a local breed or all-breed club and to participate in sanctioned matches before entering an all-breed show.

Exhibitor Tips

Equip your dog with a narrow leather show lead, which is a combination of a leash and a slide collar. For benched shows, either a bench crate or a metal-link bench chain to fasten your dog to the bench will be needed. For unbenched shows, take along your dog's crate so that he may be confined in comfort when he is not appearing in the ring. Never leave your dog in a car with all of the windows closed. In hot weather, the temperature can become unbearable in a very short time. Heat exhaustion may result from even a short period of confinement, and death may occur.

Food and water dishes will be needed, as well as a supply of food and water to which your dog is accustomed. Brushes and combs are also necessary so that your dog's coat may get a final grooming before he goes into the ring.

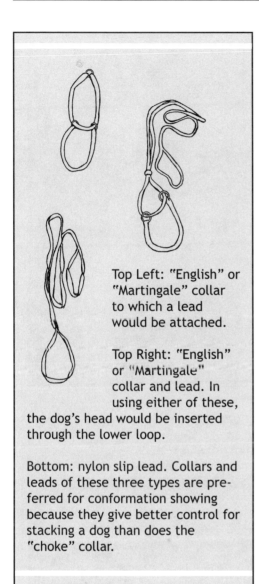

Top Left: "English" or "Martingale" collar to which a lead would be attached.

Top Right: "English" or "Martingale" collar and lead. In using either of these, the dog's head would be inserted through the lower loop.

Bottom: nylon slip lead. Collars and leads of these three types are preferred for conformation showing because they give better control for stacking a dog than does the "choke" collar.

Take along your dog's crate.

Train your young puppy to "stack" for the judge's examination.

Familiarize yourself with the schedule of classes ahead of time, because you must feed and exercise your dog and permit him to relieve himself before his class is called. Both you and your dog should be ready to enter the ring unhurriedly. Considerable skill in conditioning, training, and handling is required if your dog is to be presented properly. It is essential that you be composed, for you will transmit your nervousness to your dog.

Once the class is assembled in the ring, the judge will ask that the dogs be gaited around the ring together in a clockwise circle. If you have trained your dog well, you should have no difficulty controlling him in the ring, where he must change pace quickly and gracefully and walk and trot elegantly and proudly with his head up. The show dog must also stand quietly for examination, posing like a statue for several minutes while the judge observes his structure in detail and physically examines him. When the judge calls your dog forward for the individual examination, there should be no conversation between you and the judge unless you are asked a question.

As the judge examines the class, he measures each dog against the ideal dog described in the Standard, then rates the dogs in the ring against each other in a comparative sense and selects for first place the dog that comes closest to conforming to the Standard for its breed. You

GALLERY OF CHAMPIONS

Ch. Heartland's Louie Louie, owned by Sandy McCabe.

Ch. Coppertone Ida, TT, owned by Carole J. Nickerson.

Ch. Sir Keith of Kimvalley, an English import owned by G. Knobloch.

Ch. Heartland's Cream of the Crop, owned by Kevin and Sandy McCabe. Luke Allen photo.

Ch. Highlands Honey Dipper, owned by G. Knobloch. Photo by Kernan.

Ch. Franklin's Pickpocket for Kerrybrook, MH, owned by Christopher Wincek, was the youngest Labrador to earn both his championship and Master Hunter titles. Alverson Photo.

are expected to accept the judge's decision in a sportsmanlike manner. You have entered the show to obtain the judge's evaluation, and that is what you receive when the judge places the dogs. Good sportsmanship is a valued commodity in the show world.

OBEDIENCE COMPETITION

For hundreds of years, dogs have been used in England and Germany in connection with police and guard work, and their working potential has been evaluated through tests devised to show agility, strength, and courage. Organized training has also been popular with English and German breeders for many years, although it was practiced primarily for the purpose of training large breeds in aggressive tactics.

There was little interest in obedience training in the United States until 1933, when Mrs. Whitehouse Walker returned from England and enthusiastically introduced the sport. Two years later, Mrs. Walker persuaded the AKC to approve organized obedience activities and to assume jurisdiction over obedience rules. Since then, interest has increased at a phenomenal rate, because obedience competition is not only a sport that the average spectator can follow readily, but also a sport for which the average owner can train his dog easily. Obedience competition is suitable for all breeds. Furthermore, there is no limit to the number of dogs that may win in competition on a given day, because each dog is scored individually on the basis of a point rating system.

The dog is judged on his response to certain commands, and if he gains a high enough score in three successive trials under different judges, he wins an obedience title. Titles awarded are CD for Companion Dog, CDX for Companion Dog Excellent, and UD for Utility Dog. Two additional titles, TD for Tracking Dog and TDX for Tracking Dog Excellent, may be

won at any time. Tests for these two titles are held separately from dog shows. The qualifying score is a minimum of 170 points out of a possible 200, with no score in any one exercise less that 50 percent of the points allowed for that exercise.

Because the CD and the UD are progressive, earlier titles, with the exception of tracking titles, are dropped as a dog acquires the next higher title. If an obedience title is gained in another country in addition to the United States, that fact is signified by the word "International" followed by the title.

On July 1, 1977, the AKC approved the awarding of an additional title, Obedience Trial Champion, or OTCh. To be eligible for this title, a dog must have earned the Utility Dog title and then must have earned 100 championship points in certain types of competition, placing first three times under different judges.

In 1979, the Board of Directors of the AKC approved the test for the Tracking Dog Excellent (TDX) title. Eligibility is limited to dogs that have already earned the Tracking Dog title.

Trials for obedience-trained dogs are held at most of the larger bench shows, and obedience-training clubs are to be found in almost all communities today. Information concerning forthcoming trials is included in the *AKC Gazette* and other dog magazines. Pamphlets containing rules and regulations governing obedience competition are available upon request from the AKC and are usually available at dog shows from the show superintendent or the AKC field representative. Rules are revised occasionally, and it is your responsibility to make sure that you are training your dog under the current set of rules.

All dogs must comply with the same rules, although in the broad jump, the high jump, and the bar jump, the jumps are adjusted to the size of the breed. Classes at obedience trials are divided into Novice A and Novice B, Open A and Open B, and Utility, which is also frequently divided

OTCh. Highlands Uptown Girl, U.D.X., W.C., Can. C.D., J.H., owned by G. Knobloch.

into Utility A and Utility B. This, however, is at the option of the sponsoring club and with the approval of the AKC.

Training for Obedience

An ideal way to train your dog for obedience competition is to join an obedience class or a training club. In organized class work, beginner's classes cover pretty much the same exercises as those described in Chapter 6. However, through class work, you will develop greater precision than is possible in training the dog yourself. Amateur handlers often cause their dog to be penalized, because if you fail to abide by the rules, it is your dog that suffers the penalty. A common infraction of the rules is using more than one signal or command when regulations stipulate that only one may be used. Classwork will help eliminate such errors. Working with a class will also acquaint

both you and your dog with ring procedure so that obedience trials will not present unforeseen problems.

Thirty or forty owners and dogs often comprise a class, and exercises are performed in unison, with individual instruction provided if required. The procedure followed in training—in fact, even the wording of the various commands—may vary from instructor to instructor. Equipment used will differ somewhat, too, but will usually include a training collar and leash, a long lead, a dumbbell, and a jumping stick. The latter may be a short length of heavy dowel or a broom handle, and both it and the dumbbell are usually painted white for increased visibility.

Never take a bitch in season to a training class. Before you enroll your female dog, determine whether she may be expected to come into season before the classes are scheduled to end. If she is, it is

This Lab puppy is being trained for obedience. Here he is sitting at heel position.

Next he learns to "sit-stay" while his handler circles around him.

better to wait and enroll her in a later course, rather than start the course and then miss classes for several weeks.

In addition to the time devoted to actual work in class, your dog must have regular, daily training sessions at home. Before each class or home-training session, exercise your dog so that he will not be highly excited when the session starts. Give him the opportunity to relieve himself before the session begins. If your dog has an accident in class, it is your responsibility to clean it up. Feed your dog several hours before the time the class is scheduled to begin or else after the class is over, and never just before the training session.

Showing in Obedience

When you decide to enter your dog in obedience competition, it is well to enter a small, informal show the first time. Dogs are usually called in the order in which their names appear in the show catalog. As soon as you arrive at the show, acquaint yourself with the time schedule. If your dog is not the first to be judged, spend some time at ringside in order to observe the routine so that you will know exactly what to expect under the judge who is officiating that day.

In addition to the collar and leash, take your brushes and comb in order to give your dog a last-minute brushing before going into the ring. It is important that your dog look his best even though he is not to be judged on his appearance.

Before entering the ring, exercise your dog, give him a drink of water, and provide him with an opportunity to relieve himself. Once your dog enters the ring, he should have your full attention. Give your voice commands distinctly so that your dog will hear and understand, for there will be many distractions at ringside.

The Novice class is for dogs that have not won their CD title. In Novice A, no person who has previously handled a dog that has won a CD title in the obedience ring at a licensed or member trial, and no person who has regularly trained such a dog, may enter or handle a dog. The handler must be the dog's owner or a member of the owner's immediate family. In Novice B, dogs may be handled by the owner or by any other person.

The Open A class is for dogs that have won a CD title but not a CDX title. Obedience judges and licensed handlers may not enter or handle dogs in this class. Each dog must be handled by the owner or by a member of his immediate family. The Open B class is for dogs that have won a CD or CDX. A dog may continue to compete in this class after he has won a UD title. Dogs in this class may be handled by the owner or by any other person.

The Utility class is for dogs that have won their CDX. Dogs that have won their UD may continue to compete in this class, and dogs may be handled by the owner or by any other person. Provided the AKC approves, a club may choose to divide the Utility class into Utility A and Utility B. When this is done, the Utility A class is for dogs that have won a CDX but not a UD. Obedience judges and licensed handlers may not enter or handle dogs in this class. All other dogs that are eligible for the Utility class but that are not eligible for Utility A may be entered in Utility B.

Novice competition includes exercises such as heeling on and off lead, the stand for examination, coming on recall, the long sit, and the long down.

In Open competition, the dog must perform exercises such as heeling free, the drop on recall, the retrieve on the flat, and the retriever over the high jump. He must also execute the broad jump, the long sit, and the long down.

In the Utility class, competition includes scent discrimination, the directed retrieve, the signal exercise, directed jumping, and the group examination.

Tracking is the most difficult test. It is always done out-of-doors, of course, and, for obvious reasons, cannot be held at a dog show. The dog must follow a scent trail that is about a quarter of a mile in length. He is also required to find a scent object, such as a glove, wallet, or some

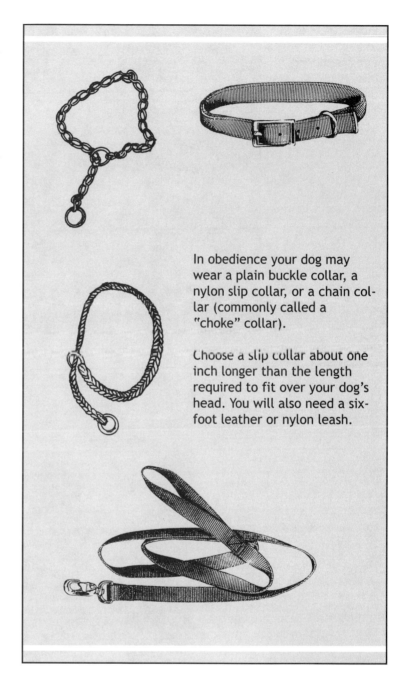

In obedience your dog may wear a plain buckle collar, a nylon slip collar, or a chain collar (commonly called a "choke" collar).

Choose a slip collar about one inch longer than the length required to fit over your dog's head. You will also need a six-foot leather or nylon leash.

other object, left by a stranger who has walked the course to lay down the scent. The dog is required to follow the trail one-half hour to two hours after the scent has been laid.

"Pierre" retrieves a dumbbell in an open obedience class. Photo © Judith Strom.

Can. Ch. Cedarwood's Minnie, J.H., Am. Can. C.D., owned by Carl and Nancy Brandow. Photo © The Standard Image, Chuck and Sandy Tatham.

THE VERSATILE LABRADOR RETRIEVER

Everyone has heard fascinating Labrador Retriever stories that show just how intelligent the breed really is. Chances are, the stories are true. For example, the New York Times ran a story on a Labrador Retriever that was hit by a car and, although injured, found his way to the veterinary clinic where he had been treated for a previous ailment. Because of the Labrador Retriever's intelligence and other qualities, such as scenting ability, endurance, and an innate desire to please, the breed is being used to help physically disabled persons, medical-assistance agencies, and law-enforcement agencies around the world.

Labrador Retrievers are used more than any other breed to provide independence for people who are blind or visually impaired. Labrador Retrievers can also serve as hearing dogs for hearing-impaired people. Labrador Retrievers are used as service dogs to assist people who have mobility limitations and as social or therapy dogs. In this capacity, the dog serves as a companion to an otherwise lonely or despondent person.

Law-enforcement and government agencies and search-and-rescue associations have long recognized the value of a well-trained dog to search for missing persons and aircraft and to assist in rescues. The Labrador Retriever also makes an excellent detection dog because he has a

This puppy is in training for Canine Companions for Independence. Photo by Bev Mager.

This guide dog helps his owner cross the street.

keen sense of smell and can detect anything from explosives to illegal drugs. Time and again, dogs have proven their exceptional ability to identify the location of agents through smell. Regardless of their assignment, they are able to work with knowledgeable handlers or owners in any setting or terrain, and virtually under any weather condition, and they have the ability to work tirelessly.

GUIDE DOGS

The Labrador Retriever is the most popular guide dog for the blind. This should not be surprising, because it has been the top registered dog with the AKC since 1991, primarily because of the breed's temperament and trainability. However, Labrador Retrievers were not the first dogs to serve as guide dogs and only recently achieved the prestigious honor of being the most popular for this work.

Guide dogs are indispensable to a sightless individual. Guide dogs help these people gain independence and complete everyday challenges like getting to work, school, or other destinations. The result is greater motility and thus self-sufficiency and self-confidence.

It is believed that the first guide dogs were trained in Germany in the early 1920s, but it was only after the middle of the century that the Labrador Retriever was used as a guide dog. Today there are at least a dozen guide-dog schools that train dogs for this work. Once the dog has been trained, the blind person is taught the proper use and handling procedures to make the dog not only his guide, but also his companion.

Guide dogs can go anywhere and therefore do not limit a blind person's access. They assist in providing access to hotels, public transportation, stores, and restaurants. Additionally, the United States and Canada have laws that prevent discrimination against a blind person. Statutory law guarantees a blind person the legal right to be accompanied by a specifically trained dog in all public accommodations and on all public transportation. A guide-dog user also has a legal right to equal housing accommodations.

Because of their intelligence, size, and ability to adapt, Labrador Retrievers are ideal as guide dogs. Perhaps the most important characteristic, however, is temperament. This breed gets along with everyone. Most of the guide-dog schools have their own breeding programs that are based on the continuance in offspring of characteristics that are considered desirable in a guide dog. Puppies are also accepted from quality stock and proven breeders as donations.

Healthy puppies are placed in homes of people who volunteer to raise the puppy. Some training schools require volunteers to participate in local programs for puppy-raisers. The volunteer family is essentially a "foster" family and must provide the puppy with love and socialization. Socialization for the puppy involves seeing the sights and hearing the sounds of everyday family activity.

At about eighteen months of age, the dog enters a comprehensive training program that lasts at least four months, although this may vary slightly from one school to another. Early training involves learning basic obedience and pulling in harness. Later the dog is taught to signal the master through the harness to lead, stop at curbs, and respond to other commands such as forward, right, and left. Correction during training is usually nothing more than a verbal reprimand. One impressive aspect of the guide dog's training are techniques that are used to cause the guide dog to disobey a command if the command when obeyed would endanger the dog's owner.

Once the dog is trained, a blind person is matched with the trained dog and the person then becomes the student for a short time. Instruction with the dog (and trainers) takes three to four weeks. The blind person learns to handle the dog and is also taught how to appreciate the guide dog's work. He or she also learns how to correct the guide dog when necessary.

The general public recognizes the importance of the guide dog to the blind person, primarily because this impressive owner/dog team is readily visible in public. The public sees the dog's work and respects the dog for his service. However, good intentions such as trying to help the blind person may actually cause problems for the guide dog and his owner. If it appears that the blind person needs help, ask before trying to assist. It is also a good idea to ask for permission before petting a guide dog.

Guide dogs are invaluable safety aids to their owners.

A pat on the head for good work!

A hearing dog alerts his owner. Photo courtesy of Hearing Dogs for the Deaf, England.

Margo Dietrich and Canine Companions for Independence Service Dog, Wallaby.

HEARING DOGS

Labrador Retrievers are popular hearing dogs for deaf people. Many breeds can work as hearing dogs, but trainers have said that because the job requires intelligence, a good disposition, and the desire to please, the Labrador Retriever is an excellent choice.

Hearing dogs are trained at schools around the world to alert their deaf owners to sounds such as a ringing telephone (textphone), alarm clock, doorbell, smoke alarm, or any sound considered to be important to the owner. The dog's effort allows a deaf person to develop increased independence and confidence. So, in addition to the practical value of the dog, there is therapeutic value as well.

Training produces a dog that will alert the deaf owner to a sound by touching him with a paw and then leading him to the source of the sound. Most dogs selected for training are donated and some come from rescue centers—organizations that find homes for abandoned or unwanted dogs so that the dog can live a happy, healthy life. If a puppy is selected for training, he must be socialized, and this becomes the responsibility of volunteers who become foster parents. During a two- to six-month period, the puppy becomes aware of and adapted to everyday family activities. Simple commands may be taught to the puppy during this time, and he is required to be a "good" family member.

At some point after socialization, formal training begins. It involves teaching the sounds that require a response and the manner in which to respond. The training program takes approximately four weeks. Finally, the dog is introduced to the new owner and further training takes place at the dog's new home.

Their friendly, outgoing disposition makes Labradors naturals for visiting nursing homes and children's wards as therapy dogs.

A Canine Companion brings his disabled partner the keys.

SERVICE, SOCIAL, AND THERAPY DOGS

There are many people who have disabilities that prevent them from doing simple day-to-day tasks. The disability may be the result of spinal muscular dystrophy, an automobile accident, or one of dozens of conditions that limit independence. Because of its intelligence and desire to please, the Labrador Retriever can be trained to become a physical extension of his owner. This dog is called a service dog, and his job is to perform tasks such as turning on a light switch or retrieving a dropped hairbrush. The person with the disability becomes more independent and self-confident with the dog's assistance and companionship.

Social and therapy dogs are trained for children or adults with developmental disabilities, for children with other disabilities, and for people who are confined and isolated from others. The social dog serves as a companion for the owner or may be used only to periodically visit such a person. Many owners suffer from loneliness, and the presence of a loving dog brings them joy. The social dog does not have many chores to perform but should be required to obey a few simple obedience commands. The Labrador Retriever excels as a social dog because of his desire to be with people and his loyalty to his master.

Therapy dogs, on the other hand, are required to learn more advanced obedience commands. Therapists have known the value of an animal in therapy programs for some time and take advantage of it. Volunteers and their trained therapy dogs visit hospitals, treatment centers, and nursing homes. The ultimate goal is to produce improvements in the patient's physical and emotional health.

Service and social/therapy puppies are selected much as the Labrador Retriever puppy is selected for show, for field trials, and for guide-dog training. Puppies are usually selected from special breeding programs or, occasionally, donated puppies may be accepted into a training program. Labrador Retrievers are frequently selected and trained.

As with dogs that will be trained for other purposes, service and social/therapy puppies require socialization before formal training begins. Volunteers take puppies into their home when the puppy is about two months old and agree to raise the puppy, providing an environment in the home that will allow the puppy to mature into a confident adult with enthusiasm for learning. These early experiences are critical. Daily routines teach the puppy how to accept strangers, ride in a car, respond to noise, and hundreds of other situations.

When the dog is about eighteen months old, he is sent to a training center. There are several centers in the United States, and their mission is to provide a better quality of life for disabled individuals through the agency of a dog. The training program may last from four to six months, depending on the dog's ability to learn.

Finally, the trained Labrador Retriever is matched with an appropriate recipient. The recipient may spend two to three weeks at the training center to learn how to use the trained dog and how to take advantage of the talents of the dog. As a result, the recipient develops increased independence and has a better outlook for the future.

DETECTOR DOGS

Agencies that must detect the presence of a variety of substances have found Labrador Retrievers to be especially valuable as detector dogs. They can be trained to find illegal drugs, gunpowder, and other explosives, accelerants, or any substance that has an odor. These dogs are used primarily by law-enforcement and government agencies but are also useful to businesses and schools. They can be used anywhere to find specific substances but may also be useful as a deterrent to minimize the presence of certain items in businesses and schools.

The Labrador Retriever is a popular choice for detector-dog training because of temperament and trainability. It goes without saying that the detector dog must have a keen sense of smell and have an outgoing, investigative attitude. A strong retrieving instinct often forms the basis for a training program for detector dogs.

The retrieving and hunting instinct is especially important during the early phases of training. This goes hand-in-hand with the dog's natural sense of curiosity and desire to please. The well-trained detector dog will alert the trainer to the scent of any contraband to which he has been conditioned and will even pinpoint the exact location. The scent can originate from a closed suitcase, from the closed trunk of a car, at the site of an arson, or just about anyplace accessible to the dog. With most detection dogs, the trainer can tell when the dog is close to making a find, because his interest is heightened, he becomes more aggressive, and he gets a "happy tail." Many are trained to "paw" at the area of the greatest scent to indicate a "find."

Dogs selected for training may be from the sporting-dog or working-dog class, but Labrador Retrievers are the favorite of many trainers. The dog should be outgoing, display a love for people, and be well-socialized. This dog should not be shy during searches in unusual situations, such as in an elevator or on a rooftop. Likewise, he should not be afraid of strange noises or people activity, such as crowds or traffic. The sex of the dog is of no consequence in selecting a Labrador Retriever to train, but he should be over one year old before serious training begins. Most handlers prefer a dog that weighs more than forty-five pounds.

The Labrador Retriever can be trained to locate practically anything. The USDA recently used a detector dog to find screwworm pupae, the immature stage of an insect that causes serious disease in cattle. The dog was able, after only five months of training, to detect screwworm-infested animals and after another three months, he could detect the screwworms pupae. The USDA has suggested using dogs at quarantine stations to decrease the possibility of reintroduction of screw-worms into eradicated areas.

More frequently, however, the dog is used to find narcotics. The list of commonly seen narcotics includes cocaine and crack, marijuana, heroin, hashish, and methamphetamines. These substances can be located in vehicles (including external parts), buildings, homes, warehouses, luggage, schools, and other areas. Because detector dogs may be used in areas where there are people, the dog should be friendly and not display the characteristics or capabilities of a protection or "bite" dog. Temperament is the main reason why Labrador Retrievers excel as detector dogs in these areas of law-enforcement and government work.

Detector dogs may also be used as deterrents to drug use. For example, many businesses contract a canine team with a specially trained dog to alert their handler to the exact location of illegal drugs on the premises. This has a significant, deterrent effect and tends to make the workplace a drug-free zone. Some schools, including universities, have found that the use of detector dogs minimizes the presence of drugs on campus and sends a message that reinforces deterrence programs.

The Labrador Retriever can be imprinted with any odor and can detect any number of scents. The dog can even discern scents that sensitive laboratory instruments cannot uncover. Many fires are suspicious and are purposefully set. The arsonist may use an accelerant to start a fire, and the detector dog will be able to

Detection or search and rescue dogs must learn to get around in difficult situations. Linda Hoffert, Red Eagle Retrievers, teaches her dog to climb a ladder.

Tracking is required as the basis for all search and rescue work.

show after the fire that an accelerant was used. The first dog used as an accelerant detector was a Labrador Retriever.

In an age of international and domestic terrorism, dogs have proven themselves to be extremely valuable in bomb detection. The idea of using a dog to detect explosives is not new and began in the military many years ago. Today, the Labrador Retriever as a bomb-detecting dog is used in airports, federal buildings, and businesses. The dog trained to detect bombs and explosives can rapidly search an airplane, motor vehicle, courtroom, or other area. Dogs can easily detect Semtex, a plastic explosive with a distinctive odor that has been used as one of the principal terrorist explosives. Semtex destroyed Pan Am Flight 103 over Lockerbie, Scotland in 1988 and was used to detonate the bomb in New York's World Trade Center bombing in 1993.

Labrador Retrievers make good explosive dogs because of their relatively passive behavior. More aggressive dogs are not wanted in a situation where excessive movement might cause detonation of a bomb. Therefore, trainers teach the dog to find the common explosive odors with a "passive response."

Other situations arise where a detector dog could be useful. The Labrador Retriever can be trained to find dead bodies (cadaver dogs). As such, they may detect body parts or the entire body. The victim may have been buried in an avalanche, may be a drowning victim, or may have been the victim of a crime. Detector dogs are usually part of a search-and-research team.

The training program for the detector dog will depend upon the scents that the dog is required to find. However, all detector dogs must ultimately want to search for a particular scent and stick with the job without getting bored or distracted. The dog selected for training must be people-oriented and must not be afraid to enter strange environments. He must also have a strong desire to search until successful. Of course, the dog must be

healthy and free of genetic defects. Most training programs take the eighteen-month-old Labrador Retriever through a three- to four-month schedule of classes to learn to detect and pinpoint a particular scent.

Most detector dogs live with the handler/trainer, who trains and works the dog. There is a strong bond between the handler and the Labrador Retriever, and this is evident when you watch the dog and handler work together. Certification is available for individuals that want to demonstrate working ability to certifying agencies. For example, the National Narcotic Detector Dog Association certifies narcotic-detector dogs.

SEARCH-AND-RESCUE DOGS

For many years, the trailing or tracking dog was the primary dog used to find missing persons. More recently, the search-and-rescue (SAR) dog that uses human scent on air currents to locate a missing person has grown in popularity. The Labrador Retriever is becoming the choice for more and more individuals involved in SAR, because the breed has the endurance, trainability, and desire to please—all of which are prerequisites for a good SAR dog.

There are many situations where a person becomes separated from others and is reported as missing. It may be a hiker lost in a remote area or an elderly person who has wandered away. Perhaps a crime victim needs assistance, or people have been trapped in rubble resulting from a terrorist's bomb like the one that exploded in Oklahoma City in 1995. SAR dogs were used extensively to find victims of the terrorists' attack on the World Trade Center in 2001. In each of these situations, the victim needs help, and it is the job of the SAR dog to help the SAR team respond to the emergency.

The primary mission of the SAR canine team is to find missing people and to save lives. Occasionally, this requires a technical rescue, such as a cliff or cave rescue, or it requires the team to perform duties related to remote-area medical care and evacuation. The trained SAR dog enhances the possibility that the missing person will be found in time whether he was in a vehicle, a boat, an aircraft, or on foot. The air-scenting dog does not need a scent article prior to searching unless the handler has trained the dog to discriminate between different human scents and wants the dog to discriminate between the scent on the article and the scents of other people working in the field. Most SAR canine teams are unpaid volunteers, although some law-enforcement and government agencies have a SAR canine team. All have specialty training and frequently take courses and workshops to update their SAR skills.

SAR associations may have to meet standards that have been set by the state for canine teams used in SAR. The handler must have the proper equipment for a basic ground search, and the dog is required to be tested under the direction of the handler. Certification is awarded when the handler and dog have demonstrated that they can work as a team to find a victim. Although the handler is important, the dog plays a major role because he must find a human scent on air currents and indicate the find to the handler.

Searches may take one of several forms, and the Labrador Retriever must be trained to respond in a variety of situations. Many searches are done in wilderness areas, meaning that the search for the missing person takes place in some remote area. Other searches are conducted in urban areas where the dog may search for missing persons in the rubble of a collapsed building. Urban searches usually follow a catastrophic disaster, such as an earthquake or a terrorist bombing.

The wilderness SAR dog works off leash and has a lot of freedom while working. He can follow at his own pace whatever scent clues are available and take shortcuts in order to find the person. Air-scenting

Rescue dogs learn to work in rubble, rocks, and water.

Indy Corson watches as his Lab, Rex, hunts for an avalanche victim in Montana. Photo © Judith Strom.

dogs can work day or night and are driven to complete the task of saving lives.

The SAR dog working an urban setting also uses air scents to locate a victim but usually works in a more confined area. The area may be a large rubble pile, and the victim may be pinned underneath layers of concrete. The dog must be able to negotiate significant obstacles such as concrete and steel to find the victim.

SAR dogs have proven to be as helpful as air-scenting dogs in other situations as well. They have located avalanche victims and have been involved in water searches. They also can find victims under ice if small holes are cut in the ice to allow scent to come through.

The Labrador Retriever selected for a SAR training program should be even-tempered and must like people. Labrador Retriever SAR dogs are not trained for protection and, therefore, are not used in criminal fugitive cases. Training for protection or as a "bite" dog requires the

Labrador Retriever to overcome his love for everyone—felon or not.

Training can start when the puppy is only eight weeks old. "Run-away" exercises where the trainer runs away from the dog teach a valuable lesson. Because of the puppy's interest and curiosity, he begins searching for the missing handler. Even at this early age, the handler is able to make decisions about the dog's trainability and his promise for success as a SAR dog. As with training for any activity, the dog should be rewarded for success, and he will be eager to continue to a higher level of training.

Once the dog has mastered the game of hide-and-seek with the handler, other people should run away and the dog encouraged to find them. These successful early lessons make difficult searches later more fun for the dog.

Finally, another person can hide and, with encouragement, the dog will begin to look for a human—any human. By this time, he will have developed the ability to use the natural instinct of finding scents on air currents and, consequently, be able to find human scents. Ultimately, the dog is trained to find the source of the scent. By the time the dog is eighteen to twenty-four months old, he should be mature enough and sufficiently trained to pass certifications.

During this training period, the handler must also learn about search and rescue. For example, he must be able to read a map to understand terrain, and must be able to indicate areas covered. Handlers must also be able to successfully navigate the terrain and use the compass. They must be able to plan a successful search and be able to communicate with other searchers via radio or telephone. Finally, the handler may want to be proficient in medical-assistance procedures.

More talented, versatile Labradors . .

Ch. Ashridge Geoffrey owned by C. Baugh catches a frisbee.

Exiting the tunnel. Photo © Judith Strom.

Labradors excell in agility competition.

Clearing a bar jump. Photo © Judith Strom.

Scaling the A-frame. Photo © Christine McHenry.

Bending through the weave poles. Photo © Christine McHenry.

Jumping through the tire. Photo © Christine McHenry.

chapter ◆ thirteen

BREEDING AND WHELPING

The breeding life of a Labrador Retriever bitch begins when she comes into season the first time at the age of eight to ten months. Thereafter, she will come into season at roughly six-month intervals. Her maximum fertility builds up from puberty to full maturity and then declines until a state of total sterility is reached in old age. It is hard to determine exactly when this occurs, because an older bitch may show signs of being in season but may not be capable of reproducing.

The length of the season varies from eighteen to twenty-one days. The first indication is a pronounced swelling of the vulva with coincidental bleeding, called "showing color," for about the first seven to nine days. The discharge gradually turns to a creamy color. During this phase, called estrus—from the tenth to the fifteenth days—the bitch is ovulating and is receptive to the male. The mature unfertilized ova survive for about seventy-two hours. If fertilization does not occur, the ova die and are discharged the next time the bitch comes into season. If fertilization does take place, each ovum attaches itself to the walls of the uterus, a membrane forms to seal it off, and a fetus develops from it.

Following estrus, the bitch is still in season until about the twenty-first day. She will continue to be attractive to males, although she will usually fight them off as

she did the first few days. Nevertheless, to avoid an accidental mating, the bitch must be confined for the entire period. Virtual imprisonment is necessary, because male dogs display uncanny abilities in their efforts to reach a bitch in season.

The odor that attracts the males is present in the bitch's urine. It is therefore advisable to take her a good distance from the house before permitting her to relieve herself. To eliminate problems completely, a veterinarian can prescribe a preparation that will disguise the odor but will not interfere with breeding when the time is right. Many fanciers use these preparations when exhibiting a bitch and find that nearby males show no interest whatsoever. It is still not advisable to permit a bitch to run loose when she had been given a product of this type, because during estrus she will seek the company of male dogs and an accidental mating may occur.

A potential Labrador Retriever brood bitch should have good bone, ample breadth and depth of ribbing, and adequate room in the pelvic region. Even though a bitch appears physically mature, breeding should not be undertaken during her first season. It should be delayed until at least the second season. Furthermore, even though it is possible for a bitch to conceive twice a year, she should not be bred more than once a year. A bitch that

Ch. Boradors Danny Boy, owned by Patricia A. Stark. Photo by B. Kurtis.

is bred too often will age prematurely, and her puppies will likely lack vigor.

Two or three months before a bitch is mated, her physical condition should be considered carefully. If she is too thin, provide a rich, balanced diet plus the regular exercise needed to develop strong, supple muscles. Daily exercise on the leash is as necessary for the too-thin bitch as for the too-fat one, although the latter will need more exercise and at a brisker pace, as well as a reduction of food, if she is to be brought to optimum condition. A prospective brood bitch must have had permanent distemper shots as well as her rabies vaccination. A month before her season is due, have your veterinarian examine a stool specimen for worms. If there is evidence of infestation, have the bitch wormed.

A Labrador Retriever dog may be used at stud from the time he reaches physical maturity well into old age. The first time a bitch is bred, it is well to use a stud that has already proven his ability by having sired other litters. The fact that a neighbor's dog is readily available should not influence the choice, because to produce the best puppies, the stud must be the most suitable from a genetic standpoint.

If the stud selected is not going to be available when your bitch is in season, you may wish to consult a veterinarian concerning medications that will inhibit the onset of the season. With such preparations, your bitch's season can be delayed indefinitely. While this is a possibility, it is not necessarily the best choice. It would be preferable to delay the mating until the next season.

Usually the first service will be successful. However, if it is not, an additional service usually is provided at no additional charge as long as the stud dog is still in the possession of the same owner. If the bitch misses, it may be because her cycle varies widely from normal. Through microscopic examination, a veterinarian can determine exactly when your bitch is

Young Labrador puppy explores in an exercise pen. Photo © Judith Strom.

Puppies enjoy the security of the whelping box and each other. Photo © Judith Strom.

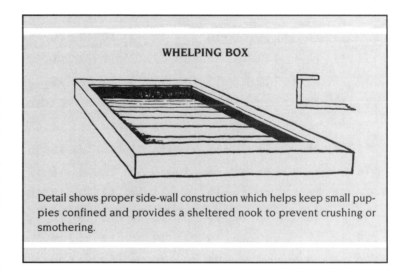

WHELPING BOX

Detail shows proper side-wall construction which helps keep small puppies confined and provides a sheltered nook to prevent crushing or smothering.

entering her estrus phase and thus is likely to conceive.

The owner of the stud should furnish a stud-service certificate, providing a four-generation pedigree for the sire and showing the date of the mating. The litter registration application is completed only after the puppies have been whelped, but it, too, must be signed by the owner of the stud as well as by the owner of the bitch. Registration forms may be obtained by writing to the AKC.

In normal pregnancy, there is usually visible enlargement of the abdomen by the end of the fifth week. By palpation, or feeling with the fingers, a veterinarian may be able to distinguish developing puppies as early as three weeks after mating, but is unwise for a novice to poke and prod in order to try to detect the presence of unborn puppies.

The gestation period normally lasts nine weeks, although it may vary from sixty-one to sixty-five days. If it goes beyond sixty-five days from the date of mating, consult your veterinarian.

During the first four or five weeks, allow your bitch her normal amount of activity. As she becomes heavier, walk her on the leash, but avoid strenuous running and jumping. Feed her a well-balanced diet, and if she becomes constipated, add small amounts of mineral oil to her food.

WHELPING

Have a whelping box prepared about two weeks before the puppies are due, and have your bitch start using it as her bed so that she will be accustomed to it by the time the puppies arrive. Preferably, the box should be square, with each side long enough so that the bitch can stretch out full length and have several inches to spare at either end. Pad the bottom with an old cotton rug or other material that is easily laundered. Tack the edges of the

Date bred (January)	Date due to whelp (March)	Date bred (February)	Date due to whelp (April)	Date bred (March)	Date due to whelp (May)	Date bred (April)	Date due to whelp (June)	Date bred (May)	Date due to whelp (July)	Date bred (June)	Date due to whelp (August)	Date bred (July)	Date due to whelp (September)	Date bred (August)	Date due to whelp (October)	Date bred (September)	Date due to whelp (November)	Date bred (October)	Date due to whelp (December)	Date bred (November)	Date due to whelp (January)	Date bred (December)	Date due to whelp (February)
1	5	1	5	1	3	1	3	1	3	1	3	1	2	1	3	1	3	1	3	1	3	1	2
2	6	2	6	2	4	2	4	2	4	2	4	2	3	2	4	2	4	2	4	2	4	2	3
3	7	3	7	3	5	3	5	3	5	3	5	3	4	3	5	3	5	3	5	3	5	3	4
4	8	4	8	4	6	4	6	4	6	4	6	4	5	4	6	4	6	4	6	4	6	4	5
5	9	5	9	5	7	5	7	5	7	5	7	5	6	5	7	5	7	5	7	5	7	5	6
6	10	6	10	6	8	6	8	6	8	6	8	6	7	6	8	6	8	6	8	6	8	6	7
7	11	7	11	7	9	7	9	7	9	7	9	7	8	7	9	7	9	7	9	7	9	7	8
8	12	8	12	8	10	8	10	8	10	8	10	8	9	8	10	8	10	8	10	8	10	8	9
9	13	9	13	9	11	9	11	9	11	9	11	9	10	9	11	9	11	9	11	9	11	9	10
10	14	10	14	10	12	10	12	10	12	10	12	10	11	10	12	10	12	10	12	10	12	10	11
11	15	11	15	11	13	11	13	11	13	11	13	11	12	11	13	11	13	11	13	11	13	11	12
12	16	12	16	12	14	12	14	12	14	12	14	12	13	12	14	12	14	12	14	12	14	12	13
13	17	13	17	13	15	13	15	13	15	13	15	13	14	13	15	13	15	13	15	13	15	13	14
14	18	14	18	14	16	14	16	14	16	14	16	14	15	14	16	14	16	14	16	14	16	14	15
15	19	15	19	15	17	15	17	15	17	15	17	15	16	15	17	15	17	15	17	15	17	15	16
16	20	16	20	16	18	16	18	16	18	16	18	16	17	16	18	16	18	16	18	16	18	16	17
17	21	17	21	17	19	17	19	17	19	17	19	17	18	17	19	17	19	17	19	17	19	17	18
18	22	18	22	18	20	18	20	18	20	18	20	18	19	18	20	18	20	18	20	18	20	18	19
19	23	19	23	19	21	19	21	19	21	19	21	19	20	19	21	19	21	19	21	19	21	19	20
20	24	20	24	20	22	20	22	20	22	20	22	20	21	20	22	20	22	20	22	20	22	20	21
21	25	21	25	21	23	21	23	21	23	21	23	21	22	21	23	21	23	21	23	21	23	21	22
22	26	22	26	22	24	22	24	22	24	22	24	22	23	22	24	22	24	22	24	22	24	22	23
23	27	23	27	23	25	23	25	23	25	23	25	23	24	23	25	23	25	23	25	23	25	23	24
24	28	24	28	24	26	24	26	24	26	24	26	24	25	24	26	24	26	24	26	24	26	24	25
25	29	25	29	25	27	25	27	25	27	25	27	25	26	25	27	25	27	25	27	25	27	25	26
26	30	26	30	26	28	26	28	26	28	26	28	26	27	26	28	26	28	26	28	26	28	26	27
27	31	27	1 (May)	27	29	27	29	27	29	27	29	27	28	27	29	27	29	27	29	27	29	27	28
28	1 (Apr.)	28	2	28	30	28	30	28	30	28	30	28	29	28	30	28	30	28	30	28	30	28	1 (Mar.)
29	2			29	31	29	1 (July)	29	31	29	31	29	30	29	31	29	1 (Dec.)	29	31	29	31	29	2
30	3			30	1 (June)	30	2	30	1 (Aug.)	30	1 (Sep.)	30	1 (Oct.)	30	1 (Nov.)	30	2	30	1 (Jan.)	30	1 (Feb.)	30	3
31	4			31	2			31	2			31	2	31	2			31	2			31	4

Whelping chart based on sixty-three day gestation period.

Venetian's Kokomo and Venetian's Classical Jazz, owned by C. Veneziano. Kokomo is co-owned with Diedre Argiro. Photo by Paw Prints.

padding to the floor of the box so that the puppies will not get caught in them and smother. Once it is obvious that labor is about to begin, cover the padding with several layers of newspapers. Then, as the papers become soiled, pull out the top layer, leaving the area clean.

Forty-eight to seventy-two hours before the litter is to be whelped, you will notice a definite change in the shape of the bitch's abdomen. Instead of looking barrel shaped, the abdomen will sag pendulously. Breasts usually redden and become enlarged, and milk may be present a day or two before the puppies are whelped. As the time becomes imminent, the bitch will probably scratch and root in her bedding in an effort to make a nest. She will refuse food and will ask to be let out every few minutes. But the surest sign is a drop in temperature of two or three degrees about twelve hours before labor begins.

The bitch's abdomen and flanks will contract sharply when labor actually starts, and for a few minutes she will attempt to expel a puppy. She will then rest for a while and try again. Someone should stay with the bitch the entire time whelping is taking place, and if she appears to be having unusual difficulties, call your veterinarian.

Puppies are usually born head first, although some may be born feet first with no

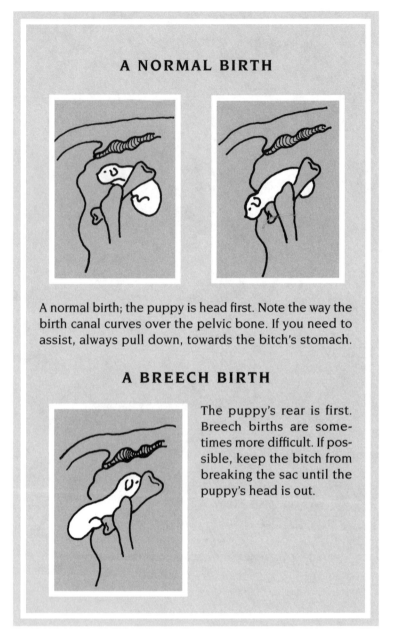

A NORMAL BIRTH

A normal birth; the puppy is head first. Note the way the birth canal curves over the pelvic bone. If you need to assist, always pull down, towards the bitch's stomach.

A BREECH BIRTH

The puppy's rear is first. Breech births are sometimes more difficult. If possible, keep the bitch from breaking the sac until the puppy's head is out.

difficulty. Each puppy is enclosed in a separate membranous sac that the bitch will remove with her teeth. She will sever the umbilical cord, which will be attached to the placenta—the soft, spongy afterbirth that is expelled right after the puppy emerges. Usually the bitch eats the afterbirth. It is therefore necessary that you make sure one is expelled with each puppy whelped. If the afterbirth is retained, the bitch may develop peritonitis and die.

The dam will lick and nuzzle each newborn puppy until it is warm and dry and ready to nurse. If puppies arrive so close together that the bitch cannot take care of them, you can help her by rubbing the puppies dry with a soft cloth. If several have been whelped but the bitch continues to be in labor, remove all but one of them and place them in a small box lined with clean towels and warmed to about seventy degrees with an electrical heating pad. The bitch will be calmer if one puppy is left with her at all times.

Whelping sometimes continues as long as twenty-four hours for a very large litter, but a litter of two or three puppies may be whelped in an hour. When the bitch settles down, curls around the puppies, and nuzzles them to her, it usually indicates that all puppies have been whelped.

Take your bitch away for a few minutes while the whelping box is cleaned and new padding is placed in it. If her coat is soiled, sponge it clean before she returns to the puppies. Once she is back in the box, offer her a bowl of warm beef broth and a pan of cool water, placing both where she will not have to get up in order to reach them. As soon as she indicates interest in food, give her a generous bowl of chopped meat to which cod-liver oil and dicalcium phosphate have been added.

If your bitch receives inadequate amounts of calcium during the period the puppies are nursing, eclampsia may develop. Symptoms are violent trembling, rapid rise in temperature, and rigidity of muscles. Veterinary assistance must be secured immediately, for death may result in a very short time. Treatment consists of massive doses of calcium gluconate administered intravenously, after which symptoms subside in a miraculously short time.

For weak or very small puppies, supplemental feeding is often recommended. Any one of three methods may be used: tube-feeding with a catheter attached to a syringe, using a doll's tiny nursing bottle, or using an eyedropper. Care must be exercised when using the eyedropper to avoid getting formula into the lungs.

The commercially prepared puppy formulas are most convenient and are readily obtainable from a veterinarian, who can also tell you which method of administering the formula is most practical in a particular case. Equipment must be kept scrupulously clean. It can be sterilized by boiling, or it can be scrubbed thoroughly and rinsed well.

All puppies are born blind, and their eyes do not open until they are ten to fourteen days old. At first the eyes have a bluish cast and appear weak. The puppies must be protected from strong light until at least ten days after their eyes open.

To ensure proper emotional development, shield young dogs from loud noises and rough handling. Being lifted by the front legs is painful and may result in permanent injury to the shoulders. When lifting a puppy, always place one hand under the chest with your forefingers between the front legs, and place your other hand under his bottom.

Flannelized rubber sheeting is an ideal surface for the bottom of the bed for new puppies. It is inexpensive and washable and will provide a surface that will give the puppies traction so that they will not slip while nursing or when learning to walk.

Sometimes the puppies' nails are so long and sharp that they scratch the bitch's breasts. Because the nails are soft, they can be trimmed with ordinary nail clippers.

WEANING

At about four weeks of age, formula should be provided. Increase the amount fed each day over a period of two weeks, when the puppies can be weaned completely. One of the commercially prepared formulas can be mixed according to the directions on the container, or you can prepare formula at home in accordance with instructions from a veterinarian. Heat the formula to lukewarm, and pour it into a shallow pan placed on the floor of the box. After his mouth has been dipped into the mixture a few times, a puppy will usually start to lap formula. All puppies should be allowed to eat from the same pan, but be sure that the small ones

Canadian Ch. West Wind Saila of Cedarwood, Am. & Can. C.D., Am. C.W.C., J.H., C.G.C., owned by David and Susan Robichaud. Photo © Chuck Tatham.

These puppies are close to weaning age. Photo © Judith Strom.

Keep fresh, clean water available at all times. Photo © Judith Strom.

Once the puppies are eating well, switch them to a good quality dry puppy chow. Feed three times a day. Photo © Kent and Donna Dannen.

get their share. If they are pushed aside, feed them separately. Permit the puppies to nurse part of the time, but gradually increase the number of meals of formula. By the time the puppies are five weeks old, the dam should be allowed with them only at night. When they are about six weeks old, they should be weaned completely. Three meals a day are usually sufficient from this time until the puppies are about three months old, when feedings are reduced to two a day. About the time the dog reaches one year of age, feedings may be reduced to one each day.

Once they are weaned, puppies should be given temporary distemper injections every two weeks until they are old enough for permanent inoculations. At six weeks, stool specimens should be checked for worms. Almost without exception, puppies become infested. Specimens should be checked again at eight weeks, and as often thereafter as necessary.

Sometimes you may decide as a matter of convenience to have your bitch spayed or your male castrated. While this is recommended when a dog has an inheritable defect or when abnormalities of reproductive organs develop, or for companion dogs, the operations automatically bar dogs from competing in shows or trials and preclude them from breeding. The operations are routine, and your dog will usually be home with you the following day.

Ch. Killingworth Tabatha Timber, owned by Lorraine Taylor of Killingworth Labrador Retrievers. Photo by Chuck Tatham.

Full sisters Ch. Franklin's Rally and Ch. Franklin's Hickory Grove, at 9 and 11 years of age. Sixteen champions were produced from this same breeding of Shamrock Acres Light Brigade and Franklin's Tally of Burrywood. Photo © Alverson.

LABRADOR RETRIEVERS IN THE UNITED STATES

The American Kennel Club recognizes 140 different breeds of purebred dogs. In 2000, the AKC registered 1,175,473 individual dogs in these various breeds. The Labrador Retriever ranked in the top ten in popularity with an annual registration of 172,841 dogs. These registration numbers attest to the great satisfaction that owners find in the breed. That the dog is an excellent companion as well as a working field dog is evident.

LABRADOR RETRIEVER

	1990	1991	1992	1993	1994	1995	1996
Totals	96,273	105,760	120,879	124,899	126,393	132,051	149,505

	1997	1998	1999	2000	2001	2002
Totals	158,366	157,936	155,046	172,841	165,970	154,616

LABRADORS EARNING SHOW AND OBEDIENCE TITLES 2000

	CH	CD	CDX	UD	UDX	OTC	TD	TDX	VST	CT
Totals	221	460	149	52	15	3	22	8	2	1

CH: Conformation Champion

CD: Companion Dog

CDX: Companion Dog Excellent

UD: Utility Dog

UDX: Utility Dog Excellent

OTC: Obedience Trial Champion

TD: Tracking Dog

TDX: Tracking Dog Excellent

VST: Variable Surface Tracking

CT: Champion Tracker

In 2000, 221 Labrador Retrievers completed their bench championship, or 0.20 percent of the total Labrador Retrievers registered that year. This does not mean, however, that the dogs were registered and finished in the same year. It does give a general comparison of the ratios between the titles earned in the breed and its total registration. The percentages for Companion Dogs were 0.12 percent, for Companion Dogs Excellent, 0.27 percent; for Utility Dogs, 0.09 percent; for Utility Dogs Excellent, 0.01 percent; for Obedience Trial Champion, 0.0017 percent; for Tracking Dogs, 0.001 percent; for Tracking Dogs Excellent, 0.005 percent; for Variable Surface Tracking 0.001; and for Champion Tracker, 0.0005 percent. The percentages for NFC were 0.001 percent; for Field Champions, 0.03 percent; for NAFC, 0.005 percent; for Amateur Field Champions, 0.02 percent; for Junior Hunters, 0.75 percent; for Senior Hunters, 0.29 percent; for Master Hunters, 0.17 percent; for Agility Novices, 0.10 percent; for Agility Opens, 0.05 percent; for Agility Excellents, 0.03 percent; for Master Agility Excellents, 0.001; for National Agility Jumper, 0.10 percent; for Open Agility Jumper 0.05 percent; and for Excellent Agility Jumper, 0.04 percent.

LABRADOR RETRIEVER BREEDERS

There are many kennels that breed and show Labrador Retrievers today, and still others that were once prominent but are no longer operating. The kennels that are included here are those that have been the most active in the last thirty years. The following list of kennels is in alphabetical order either by kennel prefix or by the owner's name.

ADIDAS KENNEL, located in Silver Spring, Maryland, was founded by Marci Swan in 1973. In addition to Labrador Retrievers, Ms. Swan raises Great Danes. Foundation stock for this kennel carries the Sandylands bloodlines. Obedience training as well as bench conformation are treated in this kennel, as evidenced by the list of winners. These include: Ch. Adidas Johnny Unitas, CD; Ch. Adidas Jeep; Ch. Monsev Ask an Architect, CD; Ch. Monsev Ask an Anthropologist, CD; and Celebration's Char-Koll.

Mrs. Richard M. Oster founded her **AJOCO KENNEL** in Barrington, Rhode Island, in 1970. Mrs. Oster imported her foundation stock from England. She started with Mansergh bloodlines, then

FIELD TITLES 2000

	FIELD				HUNTER				AGILITY					
	NFC	FC	NAFC	AFC	JH	SH	MH	AN	AO	AE	MAE	NAJ	OAJ	EAJ
Totals	2	51	8	39	1,301	516	303	182	101	49	19	179	79	53

NFC: National Field Champion

FC: Field Champion

NAFC: National Amateur Field Champion

AFC: Amateur Field Champion

JH: Junior Hunter

SR: Senior Hunter

MH: Master Hunter

AN: Agility Novice

AO: Agility Open

AE: Agility Excellent

MAE: Master Agility Excellent

NAJ: National Agility Jumper

OAJ: Open Agility Jumper

EAJ: Excellent Agility Jumper

American and Canadian Ch. Chelons Teton of Redrock, C.D., owned by Barbara Saurin. Photo by Missy Yuhl.

later added bitches from Sandylands. Two English imports that became American champions are Ch. Mansergh Moose and Ch. Mansergh Merry Gentleman. Homebreds include Ch. Ajoco's Lillymere and Ch. Ajoco's Damn Yankee. Other dogs in this kennel are Ch. Eireannach Black Angus, Ch. Eireannach Black Coachman, Ch. Jayncourt Fantasy, and Ch. Janycourt Follow Mee.

ALLEGHENY KENNEL was established in Keezletown, Virginia, in 1968 by Clare Senfield. The foundation stud dog was Ch. Allegheny McDuff. The breeding program was based on the bloodlines of the Mansergh Kennel from England. This kennel produced Ch. Allegheny's Live Spark, CD; Ch. Allegheny Bezique; Ch. Allegheny's Eclipse, Allegheny's Tudor Knight, JH; and Am. Can. Ch. Allegheny's Sugarplum, who went Best of Breed at the 1994 Canadian National Specialty.

AMALGAMATED RETRIEVERS was established by James D. Dessen, DDS, in Saint Paul, Minnesota, in 1975. This field kennel lists FC, AFC, and CFC Triple Echo as its foundation stud dog.

AMA'S LABRADOR RETRIEVERS was established in 1970 by Don and Rhoda Zapetello in Hollywood, Florida. All breeding stock goes back to Aust. Ch. Sandylands Tan. Winners from this kennel are Ch. Ama's Houhyhnm Gift of Hope, Ch. Anderscroft Roustabout, Ch. Novacroft Clas-

AFC, CFC, and CAFC Chugach Hills Jazz's Rascal, owned by Larry and Anna Calvert.

sicway Came Dancing, Ch. Novacroft Carlos, and Ch. Roseacre Blackberry.

Ms. Janet Stolarevsky established her **AMBERSAND LABRADORS** in Dexter, Michigan. Being a schoolteacher, Ms. Stolarevsky limits her breeding program to summer vacations, although she does show throughout the year. Her breeding stock was primarily from Shamrock Acres Kennel with some outcrossing to the English Viscum and Ardmarglia bloodlines. The top dog in this kennel is Ch. Timmbrland Golden Star, who won 8 Best in Shows, 32 Group Firsts, and 131 Best of Breeds. He was also top Labrador Retriever in 1977 and 1978. Another consistent winner at this kennel is Am. Can. Ch. Rorschach's Royal Flush.

The **ASHRIDGE KENNEL** has been located in Lansing, New York, since 1981. The owner, Carol A. Baugh, imported her foundation bitch, Fredwell Bridget, from England in 1977. This kennel produced Am. Can. Ch. Ashridge Clementine; Am. Can. Ch. Ashridge Lancelot, co-owned with Rose Marie Duerr; Ch. Ashridge Maryleone, CD, JH; Ch. Ashridge Admiral Wager, CD; and Ashridge Lindesfarne, WC, JH.

In 1962, Allan and Jeanne Young founded their **BALMORAL LABRADORS** in

Franklin, Massachusetts. Foundation stud Ch. Balmoral's Golden Nugget is a grandson of Eng. Am. Can. Ch. Balmoral's Fergus; Am. Can. Ber. Ch. Labradale Jill of Balmoral; Ch. Tippecanoe Trail Sunset; Can. Ch. Balmoral's Blackout Jerry; and Can. Ch. Balmoral's Brigadoon Duke.

BAR/NONE LABRADORS was founded in 1988 by Michael and Shari Jones in Pueblo, Colorado. Foundation stock was AFC Bar/None Shaydee Laydee. Other dogs from this kennel are Bar/None's Double Didget, Bar/None's Classy Chassis, and Trieven Touch of Class.

Dr. Keith S. Grimson established his **BAROKE KENNEL** in Durham, North Carolina, in 1965. Foundation dogs were Ch. Harrowby Baron, Ch. Harrowby Storm, and Ch. Sandylands Mona Lisa. Dr. Grimson limits his kennel to no more than seven dogs and breeds only about one litter per year. The first homebred champion was Ch. Baroke Yellow Jacket, who won his championship in 1967, followed by Ch. Baroke All Hallows Eve, who became a champion in 1968. Other homebreds include Am. Can. Ch. Baroke Statesman, Ch. Baroke Ginger, and Ch. Baroke Cindy. Other dogs bred by this kennel but finished by new owners include Ch. Baroke Honey B of Willohaven, CD; Ch. Baroke Heidi Ann, CDX; Ch. Baroke Spokesman, CDX; and Ch. Baroke Jim G.

DENNIS BATH of Belleville, Illinois, has been in field-trial Labrador Retrievers since 1968. He co-owned the 1979 and 1980 NAFC and FC Lawhorn's Cadillac Mac with Gerald Lawhorn. This dog won the National Amateur Retriever Championship at four and one-half years of age in 1979. In the 1979 trial season, he won a total of seventy-three All Age points, all before he was five years old.

BIGSTONE KENNEL is owned by Bill and Louise Rook of Beardsley, Minnesota. Operating since 1944, this long-established field-trial kennel has bred many winners. The list includes the 1962 National Retriever Champion, FC Bigstone Hope; FC Bigstone Bandit; FC Bigstone

Scout; AFC Bigstone Shady Lill, and Dual Ch. Matchmaker For Deer Creek.

Gary Ahlgren and Mary Williams-Ahlgren started their **BLACK OAK KENNEL** in 1988 in Winters, California. Two of their winning dogs include FC, AFC Hightest CC Waterback, MH and FC, AFC Ornbaunk's Buck Wheat, MH.

C. L. and Jan Hutchmacher established their **BLUFF SPRING KENNEL** in Grand Tower, Illinois, in 1976. This field-trial kennel breeds three to five litters a year, all on champion stock. The foundation stud is FC Win-Toba's Majestic Lad.

BRAEMAR KENNEL was established in Santa Rosa, California, in 1974 by Jane R. Borders. The foundation stock is represented with Ch. Elysium's Chelsea O'Neill, CD, WC and Ch. Braemar Heather, CDX, WC. More than two dozen Labrador Retrievers carrying the Braemar prefix have earned their titles either as bench champions or with certificates for obedience, tracking, or working. Among the winners are: Ch. Braemar Duggan, the Best-of-Breed winner at the 1979 Labrador Retriever Club National Specialty; Ch. Braemar's Oakmead Dillon, CD, WC; Ch. Broomier Drake, CD, WC; Ch. Braemar Castlecrag, WC; and Braemar's Trick or Treat, CD, TD.

Ceylon and Marjorie Brainard located their **BRIARY KENNEL** in Alderwood Manor, Washington, in 1962. The foundation stud for this kennel was Ch. Lockerbie Brian Boru, WC, who is the sire of more than fifty champions. This dog combined the Sandylands and Blaircourt lines. Among the many dogs carrying the Briary name are: Ch. Briary Trace of Brian, CD; Ch. Briary Abbey Road; Ch. Briary Bandolier; and Ch. Briary's Glencoe Mac Brain.

CAMPBELLCROFT LABRADORS was established by Donald and Virginia Campbell in Soquel, California, in 1974. Their foundation bitch was Ch. Agber Daisy of Campbellcroft, CD, WC. Her first litter produced Ch. Campbellcroft's Pede, CD, WC; and Campbellcroft's Piper, CDX, WC, and another bitch that was donated to the Guide Dogs for the Blind. Am. Can.

Ch. Chelon's Mac the Knight, J.H., W.C., owned by Fran Ippensen and Pat Brannock. Photo by Bill Meyer.

Ch. Coalcreeks Gimme A Break, owned by George and Lillian Knobloch.

Kingsdale's Midas Touch, owned by Diane MacMillan. Mikron Photos.

Ch. Campbellcroft's Angus, CD, WC, a Best-in-Futurity winner at the National Specialty in 1978, won Best of Breed at the National in 1987 from the Veteran's Class. Two of his daughters are Ch. Harrington Campbellcroft Lass, JH, WC and Ch. Breton Gate Cairngorm, CD, JH, WC.

Nancy and Carl Brandon located their **CEDARWOOD KENNEL** in Bradford, Maine, in 1978. This kennel has produced the following winners both on the bench and in the field: Am. Can. Ch. Cedarwood's Spice 'n Thyme, JH, WCX, TDI, CWCI; Am. Can. Ch. Plantier's Ruthless Ruthie, MH, CD, WCX; and Can. Ch. West Wind Saila of Cedarwood, Am. Can.

CD, CWC, JH, CGC. The following two dogs are pet therapy dogs: Ch. West Wind Winchester, JH, AWC, CWC, TDI and Am. Can. Ch. Cedarwood's Sable, JH, AWC, CWC, TDI.

CHUCKLEBROOK KENNEL has been located in Burlington, Connecticut, since 1967 and is owned by Leslie and Diane Pilbin. The foundation bitch was Ch. Spenrock's Bohemia Champagne, who has been a top producer and was winner of the Brood Bitch Class at the National Specialty in 1978. Winners from Chucklebrook Kennel include Ch. Chucklebrook Helen; Ch. Chucklebrook Champagne Mist; Ch. Chucklebrook Tuc O'Aspetuck;

Ch. Chucklebrook Peerybingle, UD, WC; Am. Can. Ber. Ch. Chucklebrook Winterset Marks, CD, WC; Can. Ch. Chucklebrook Crusader; Ch. Chucklebrook Mousefeathers; Ch. Chucklebrook Rand's Supr Savr; and Ch. Chucklebrook Kira O'The Mist.

COCHISE LABRADORS was founded in 1970 in Tucson, Arizona, by Charles and Salle McNeil. The foundation stock for this kennel included Ch. Cochise Bushwacker and Ch. Wingmasters Tiara of Cochise. Interest in obedience is also stressed here, with Driftwood's Sundance Kid, CD and King Midas Gold of Cochise, CD.

Barbara Hogan's **COULD BE KENNEL** was established in Grandview, Missouri, in 1957. Ms. Hogan has bred more than three dozen champions and finished a number of other dogs of which she was not the breeder. Her foundation dogs were Ch. Mighty Manfred of Maryglo, CD and Ch. Beer's Mug, CD. Among dogs carrying the kennel prefix are Ch. Could Be's Encore, Ch. Could Be's Haven Rock, Ch. Could Be's Black Angus Heifer, Ch. Could Be's Gold Dust, and Ch. Could Be's Moon Dust. Ms. Hogan also bred and showed Clumber Spaniels.

CREOLE KENNEL has been located in Shreveport, Louisiana, since 1962. This field-trial kennel is owned by Mr. and Mrs. Donald P. Weiss. Winners include: NFA and AFC Creole Sister; FC, AFC Creole Carpetbagger; FC, AFC Creole Ducksoup; FC, AFC Macaroilyn's Feather Tiger; and AFC Oak Lahoma's Redpath Smith.

Debi and Kenny Richardson established their **DEBKEN'S KENNEL** in Grain Valley, Missouri, in 1980. Their foundation bitches were Ch. Beavercreeks Trey's A Charm, CGC, CD and Woodgate's Little Miss Tish, CD. Other winners from this kennel are: Ch. Deb's Tag A Long, CGC, CDX; Am. Can. Ch. Debken's Scorcher of a Knight, TD, CGC; and Ch. Clearlake's Sparks Will Fly, CGC.

DELIGHT LABRADORS was established in Shirley, New York, by Mr. and Mrs. Phillip Parr. The foundation bitch, Parr's Midnight Delight, was followed by Ch. Aquarius Parr's Delight, who produced Ch. Delight Creme De Menthe. This kennel also produced a bitch for the guide-dog program on Long Island. In addition to Labrador Retrievers, the Parrs also raise Cavalier King Charles Spaniels and Border Terriers.

Pete and Tanya Rothing established their **DIAMOND R KENNEL** in Bozeman, Montana, in 1982. Their foundation bitch was Diamond R Sexy Sophie, JH. Her son, Diamond R Randy Renegade, MH, became the first Master Hunter in Montana. Other dogs bred by this kennel are: AFC Valtor's O.C. Pete; Diamond R Waterfowl Biddy, MH; Diamond R Flash Dance, MH; Freezout Diamond Girl, MH; and Skookum Kennebee Jess, MH.

ELDEN'S LABRADOR RETRIEVERS is owned by Elden Williams of Milwaukie, Oregon. Mr. Williams has campaigned his Ch. Elyod's Macbeth of Canterbury to rank as the top sporting dog in the West and one of the all-time great winning Labrador Retrievers. Macbeth's son, Ch. Elden's Tigger Too, carries on the winning ways of his sire.

ERINS EDGE LABRADORS was established in Richfield, Wisconsin, in 1980 by Nancy Planasch. This kennel specializes in breeding chocolate Labrador Retrievers. Current working dogs include Roadhouse Gusto and Mallard Lake Lady Magnum.

Bill Fabian located his **FABIAN'S RETRIEVER TRAINING KENNEL** in North Branch, Minnesota, in 1972. Dogs representative of this kennel are: FC, AFC Triple Echo; FC, AFC Camelot's Sir Lancelot III; FC, AFC Black Jack Ray's Double; FC, AFC Rumba's Rain Dancer; and FC, AFC Ms Mischief Magic Marker.

JIM FALKNER is a retired obedience judge from Richardson, Texas. In addition to Labrador Retrievers, Mr. Falkner has shown Pembroke Welsh Corgis in both bench and obedience competition and pointers in field trials. His original Labrador Retriever stock was of Bigstone and Medlin breeding. Winners from this kennel are: Ch. Sudrok's Don Polo, UD;

Reneway Maudie of Ashridge, C.D., J.H., owned by C. Baugh.

Ch. Highlands Bronze Chieftain, owned by G. Knobloch. Photo by W. Bushman.

Toothacres Booger Red, CDX; and Falkner's Candy Bar, UD.

FRANKLIN LABRADORS was established in Franklin, Michigan, in 1951 by Mrs. B. W. Ziessow, the wife of judge Dr. Bernard W. Ziessow. Among their sixty-five champions are: BIS Ch. Dark Star of Franklin; Ch. Golden Chance of Franklin; FC Discovery of Franklin; Am. Can. Ch., FC Franklin's Tall Timber; and Ch. Tabatha's Dodena of Franklin, CD, TD, WC.

M. C. McGee established **GREY DAWN LABRADORS** in Wichita Falls, Texas, in 1983. Foundation stock is represented by FC Mick the Quick; Pacer's Prancer of Grey Dawn, JH; and Grey Dawn's Sho-Nuf Sister, CD, JH. Kennel winners include: Grey Dawn's Uptown Andy Brown, CD, JH; Grey Dawn's Dyna-Might Do It, MH; Grey Dawn's Biscuits 'N Gravy, SH; and Grey Dawn's Black Jack Mac, JH.

Ms. Eileen Ketcham established her **GROVETON KENNEL** in West Lebanon, New York, in 1965. Among the original breeding stock were Ch. Springfield's Cheshire Cheese, Ch. Carefree of Keithray, and Lady Tinkerbelle of Groveton. Winners carrying the kennel prefix include: Am. Can. Ber. Ch. Grovetons Apollo Moon Dust, Ch. Grovetons Copper Buck Shot, Ch. Grovetons Winjammer, and Ch. Grovetons Shashane.

George and Lillian Knobloch opened their **HIGHLAND KENNEL** in Howell, New Jersey, in 1975. Among this kennel's winners are: Ch. Highlands Bronze Chieftain; Am. Can. Ch. Highlands Chivas Regal; Ch. Sir Keith of Kimvalley; Ch. Highlands Space Ranger; Ch. Highlands California Cooler; and OTCh. Highlands Uptown Girl, UDX, Can. CD, WC, JH, who earned multiple High in Trials and Combined High in Trials.

The **HURRICANE KENNEL** of Mr. and Mrs. Don H. Gearheart has been located in Royal Oak, Maryland, since 1945. This field-trial kennel is represented with the following list of winners: FC Zipper's Dapper Sapper; FC Zoe; FC Netley Creek Black Brute; FC Sassy Sioux of Tukwila, CD; and AFC Blackfoot Lobo.

INDIAN VALLEY KENNEL was founded in 1958 in Mount Vernon, Iowa, by Jeanne M. Koch. Breeding stock

Ch. Franklin's Champagne, owned by Mrs. B. W. Ziessow. Booth Photograpy.

included the bitch Altiora of Blaircourt from Scotland and Ch. Harrow by Leslie. Dogs representing this kennel include: Ch. Indian Valley Roisin Dubb, Ch. Indian Valley Raed Wulf, Ch. Indian Valley Roy Roy, and Ch. Indian Valley Buff.

IRONPRIDE LABRADORS are from the Delta Crown Kennel of Mount Morris, Michigan. Winners from this kennel are: Ch. Ironpride's Delta Dignity, Ch. Ironpride's Pacesetter, Ch. Ironpride's Hi-Tide Dictator, and Ch. Delta's Kinley Crocker.

JAZZTIME KENNEL was founded by Larry and Anna Calvert in Charlo, Montana. Their breeding program was based on FC, AFC, CFC, CAFC Jazztime,

MH. Other dogs at this kennel are: AFC, CFC, CAFC Chugach Hills Jazz's Rascal and GMHR Chugach Hills Itsy Bitsy. Dogs bred here but sold to others include: FC Chugach Hills Montana Jazz, and FC Jazztime's Alaskan Rendezvous.

Juxi Burr located her **JUSTES B KENNEL** in Albuquerque, New Mexico, in 1966. Starting primarily with field stock, this kennel has expanded its breeding program to include show and obedience dogs. Winners include: Ch. Shamrock Acres Justes B Chile; Ch. Justes Donau Bush's Charger, CDX, TD; Ch. Aristes' Justes B Torpedo, CD; Justes Tar and Nicotine, CD; and Justes B Final Decision, CD.

KILLINGWORTH LABRADOR RE-TRIEVERS was established in 1959 by Lorraine Robbenhaar and is located in Harrison, Maine. Dogs carrying the Killingworth prefix are: Ch. Killingworth's Thunderson, a sire of twenty-six champions; Ch. Clemmson of Killingworth, a Westminster Best-of-Breed winner in 1982; Ch. Killingworth Tabatha Timber; and the English import, Ch. Kupros Sparctacus.

KOOLAU KENNEL is located in Waimanolo, Hawaii. Its leading stud is BIS Ch. Prince Charlie Iliokai. Other winners include Ch. Healani Alii O'Koolau and Malie Alii O'Koolau, CDX.

John J. and Judith M. Timmons located their **LABRADOR LANE KENNEL** in Tucson, Arizona, in 1969. Breeding stock included Am. Can. Ch. Silvershoe Golden Shane, CD; Caramela de Labrador Lane, Am. Can. CD, Mex. PC; and Zambito Negro De Centavo, CD. Other winners in the kennel are Ch. Aymes of Annie of Broadfen; Picara, CDX, Mex. P.C., W.C.; Zorro de Labrador Lane, Am. Can. CD, and Mex. P.C.; and Am. Can. Mex. Ch. Lynn's Folly.

Lloyd Moore's **LODI KENNEL** was established in 1971 in West Paducah, Kentucky. In addition to Labrador Retrievers, the kennel breeds Golden Retrievers. Basically a training kennel, Lodi has trained FC Madam Queen II, and FC Glen's Black Jack.

Lisa DeSilva started her **MARIT LABRADORS** in Santa Rosa, California, in 1992. Her foundation bitch was SR Yellow Rose of Marit, JH, CGC. This bitch is in hunting tests and is a social therapy dog. Her first litter was sired by Ch. Raintree Slippery When Wet, JH, CGC.

PINETREE KENNEL, now located in Oklahoma City, Oklahoma, was founded in 1973. Foundation stock included Ch. Shamrock Acres Yankee Doodle II, CD; Shamrock Acres Happy Talk; and Springfield's Victoria. The relocation of the kennel has slowed the breeding program, but work here continues in both conformation and obedience.

RAVENWOOD KENNEL, owned by Bachman Doar, Jr., of Richmond, Virginia, dates from 1970. This kennel is essentially for training and handling. Among the winners are: FC, AFC Denham's Delta Chief; FC Buckshot Gus; FC Westwind Supernova Chief; and FC, AFC Blue Water Brigadier.

RIDGE VIEW LABRADOR RE-TRIEVERS was located in Elkader, Iowa, in 1977 by Donna Rice. While Ms. Rice put an obedience title on a dog in 1974, she did not get her foundation bitch, Ridge View Happy Girl, until 1977. Dogs carrying the kennel prefix are: Ch. Ridge View Gentleman Jack; Ch. Pine Edge Ridge View Snobear; Ch. Ridge View Home Fire Burning; and Ch. Ridge View Gust O'Wind. Other winners include: Ch. Honorbright Mischief Mandy and Honorbright Ocean Breeze, CD.

ROYAL OAK KENNEL was established by Mitchel P. Brown in Monticello, Georgia, in 1972. Besides Labrador Retrievers, the kennel raises Flat-Coated Retrievers. Winners from this kennel include: FC, AFC Esprit Playin' for Keeps, and AFC Esprit Hard Ball.

RUPERT KENNEL was established by Dorothy Howe in 1941. One of the first litters produced Ch. Rupert Dahomey, Ch. Rupert Daphne, and Ch. Rupert Desdemona. This litter was from both field and bench heritage. Later champions were Ch. Rupert Marleigh Bingham; Ch. Rupert Jurisprudence; Ch. Rupert Searchon; and Ch. Rupert Brookhavens Angell, CD. In addition to being a top breeder for more than a quarter of a century, Ms. Howe is also the author of *This is the Labrador Retriever*, which was published in 1972.

Dick Plantier established his **RUTH-LESS RETRIEVERS OF NEW HAMP-SHIRE** in Bedford, New Hampshire, in 1989. Foundation stock is represented by MHR, Am. Can. Ch. Plantier's Ruthless Ruthie, CD, WDX, MH. Winners carrying this kennel prefix are: Ruthless' Ms. Chievious Heidi, CDX, SH; and Ruthless' Blazing Brentley, WCI, JH; and Ruthless' Scalawags Scarlett, WC, JH.

Ch. Boradors Danny Boy, owned by Patricia A. Stark.

Modesto, California, has been the home of the **SAILIN LABRADORS** of Art and Beth Davis since 1974. Winners are Ch. Star's Sailerman of Seasac, CDX, WC; Am. Can. Ch. Elysium's Sailin Cat Ballou; and Sailins Wily Wind Song. The Davises maintain an active interest in bench, obedience, and field work, and start training their dogs on wings and water at seven weeks of age.

SCHOMER KENNEL of Joe and Lee Schomer is located in Conroe, Texas. This field-trial kennel, established in 1962, also raises Golden Retrievers. Winners from this kennel include 1957 and 1959 NFC Spirit Lake Duke; the 1972 AFC, NFC Royal's Mooses Moe; FC, AFC, CFC Rocky Road of Zenith; FC, AFC Smokey of Park Zenith; FC, AFC Royal Oaks Super Stuff; and FC, AFC Hoss of Palm Grove.

SHERWIN SCOTT'S kennel is located in Phoenix, Arizona. His top-winning Labrador Retriever was the 1994 winner NAFC, FC Ebonstar Lean Mac.

SCRIMSHAW KENNEL of John and Barbara Barfield of Meredith, New Hampshire, dates from 1962. Scrimshaw was originally known as Spindrift Kennel. A second breed at the kennel is the Smooth Fox Terrier. Original Labrador Retriever breeding stock was of the Aldenholme bloodlines, which go back to Arden, Deer Creek, and Timber Town kennels. At Scrimshaw are the English imports Ch. Jayncourt Follow Mee and Ch. Sandylands Crystal, and homebreds Ch. Scrimshaw Another Deacon, Ch. Scrimshaw Blue Nun, a group winner from the classes and the top bitch for 1979, and Ch. Scrimshaw Grainne Ne Mhaille. Scrimshaw Clearly An Angel was sold to Mr. and Mrs. D. Meredith, under whose ownership she earned the tracking title at one year and thirteen days of age. Scrimshaw Ocean Born Mary, owned by Mr. and Mrs. P. Sobolewski, brought in forty pheasants in her ninth year, in spite of being deaf.

SHAMROCK ACRES KENNEL of Mrs. Sally B. McCarthy was located in Waunakee, Wisconsin, in 1957. This is undoubtedly the kennel that has had the greatest effect on the breed in the last thirty years. More than 500 bench champions, 500 obedience-trial winners, and 50 field champions carry the Shamrock Acres prefix in their names. Foundation bitches

Ch. Aquarius Parr's Delight, owned by Sharon and Philip Parr.

Ch. Highlands California Cooler, owned by G. W. Knobloch. Photo © K. Booth Photography.

for Mrs. McCarthy were Ch. Whygin Campaign Promise, dame of seventeen champions; Ch. Whygin Gentle Julia of Avec, dam of thirteen champions; and Ch. Whygin Busy Belinda, dam of eleven champions. The leading sire in the history of the breed and a record-setting BIS winner was Ch. Shamrock Acres Light Brigade, who sired almost 100 champion get. Am. Can. Ch. Shamrock Acres Sonic Boom is the sire of more than thirty champions. Ch. Shamrock Acres Cotton Candy, owned by Mrs. James Getz, was the dam of twelve champions. Other leading producers from Shamrock Acres are BIS Ch. Shamrock Acres Casey Jones, CD; Ch. Shamrock Acres One Way Ticket; Ch. Shamrock Acres Someday Sue, CD; Ch. Shamrock Acres Donnybrook; and Ch. Shamrock Acres Royal Wag.

SHENANDOAH KENNEL was established in Radford, Virginia, in 1970 by Kenneth and Doreen Anderson. Among the winners from this kennel are Am. Can. Ber. Ch. Shenandoah Sea Sprite, Ch. Shenandoah Spritely Diana, Ch. Shenandoah Ebon Echo, and Shenandoah Jet Lady, WC.

Janet Churchill's **SPENROCK KENNEL** of Chesapeake City, Maryland, dates from 1956. In addition to Labrador Retrievers, Ms. Churchill raises Rottweilers. Her foundation Labrador Retriever stock included Eng. Am. Ch. Lawnwoods Hot Chocolate, who qualified in the field and won two BIS awards before being exported. In the United States he became a Group winner and was Best of Breed at a specialty. Other foundation dogs are Int. Ch. Spenrock Banner, WC; Ch. Rivermist Tweed of Spenrock; and Ch. Spenrock Heatheredge Mariner. These dogs represent the English breeding lines of Sandylands, Heatheredge, and Bally-Duff. Among the winners bred by this kennel are Ch. Spenrock Cajun, Ch. Spenrock Ambassador, Ch. Spenrock Top Gallant, and Ch. Spenrock's Bohemia Champaign.

SOUTH BAY KENNEL was established in 1956 in Easton, Maryland, by August and Louise V. Belmont. The kennel originally started with Chesapeake Bay Retrievers and gradually shifted to Labrador Retrievers until 1970, when the change was complete. The great Labrador Retriever winner of this kennel is the 1968 NFC

Winning Highest Scoring Dog in Trial is Wanapum War Bonnet, U.D., owned by Mrs. David L. Taylor. Don Petrulis Photography.

and 1967 and 1968 NAFC Super Chief, who so prominently figures in pedigrees of winning field dogs today. A full brother of Super Chief is FC, AFC Carr-Lab Penrod, and a son of Super Chief is FC, AFC Air Express. Other winners are Dual Ch. Bomarc of South Bay, CD; AFC Carr-Lab Raider's Gain; and FC, AFC Wanapum Lucky Yo Yo. These dogs have been handled exclusively by one or both of the Belmonts.

The SPRINGFIELD KENNEL of Mrs. R. V. Clark, Jr., is located in Middleburg, Virginia. This kennel has a long and outstanding record in the showring, both with dogs carrying the kennel prefix and with non-Springfield-bred dogs. National Specialty winners include Ch. Springfield's Musette and Eng. Am. Ch. Kimvalley Picklewitch. Veteran Class winners at the Specialty include Eng. Am. Ch. Kenbara Jill,

Ch. Breton Gate Cairngorm, C.D., J.H., W.C., winning Best Veteran in Sweepstakes at the 1994 Labrador Retriever Club of American national specialty. Owners are Donald and Virginia Campbell. Photo by Callea.

the dam of fourteen champions, and Ch. Springfield's Miss Willing. Ch. Madras Brandlesholme Sam's Song was a Best-of-Breed winner at Westminster Kennel Club, where he also placed in Group.

Jim and Mary Hankins established their **STARLINE KENNEL** in Rockford, Illinois, in 1970. Ch. Ham's Better Check and Ch. White Buck of Starline represent the foundation stock. Winners carrying the kennel name are: Ch. Starline Timm Buck Too; Ch. Starline Night Light; Ch. Starline Special Occasion, owned by Greg and Diane Wehrheim; Ch. Starline Mecca of Timm-

brland, owned by Roy and Faye Timm; and Ch. Starline Marty, owned by Bruce Martindale.

STEDENMAR KENNEL of Martha Jo Willard was established in 1972 in Tuskegee, Alabama. Ms. Willard put her breeding program on hold while she attended veterinary medicine school. She carried on only a limited breeding program. Her foundation dogs were Ch. Forecast Bowdoin and Forecast Scripps, CD.

Patricia A. Stark has owned **STONEY-GATE KENNEL** in Columbus, Ohio, since 1962. From 1962 until 1980, her principal breed was the German Shepherd. The first Labrador Retriever for this kennel was Ch. Boradors Danny Boy, the sire of nine champions. Among his get are Ch. Teton of Redrach and Can. Ch. Woodhaven's Irish Mist. He also produced an Avalanche Dog for the Park City Ski Patrol in Utah.

Dr. and Mrs. John Ippensen maintain their **SUNNYBROOK ACRES KENNEL** in Springfield, Missouri. In addition to Labrador Retrievers, the Ippensens have raised English Springer Spaniels and Irish Setters. Foundation stock for the Ippensen's Labrador Retrievers is of the Shamrock Acres bloodlines, although crossing has been made to English lines. Ch. Sunnybrook Acres Sandpiper is a Group winner. Other winners from this kennel are Ch. Sunnybrook Acres Cinderella, Ch. Sunnybrook Acres Solitaire, Ch. Sunnybrook Acres Black Gold, Ch. Sunnybrook Acres Hot Cocoa, and Ch. Heatherbrook's Could Be Jazzy. The leading winner from this kennel is Am. Can. Ber. Bah. Ven. S.A. Dom. Ch. Sunnybrook Acres Ace O'Spades, Can. Dom. CD, P.R. Ven. Ber. CDX, Ber. TD, Bah. UD, Am. UD, TX, WC, an all-breed Best-in-Show and Specialty Best-of-Breed winner.

Richard C. Weiner located his **SUNNYVIEW LABRADORS, INC.**, in Salem, Oregon, in 1965. Foundation stock include: FC Anzac of Zenith; NFC, AFC San Joaquin Honcho; GMHR Sunnyview's Royal Coachman, MH; NAFC, FC, CNFC CAFC Piper's Pacer; and GMHR Sunnyview's King of Spades, MH. Among the many winners from this kennel are: GMHR, WR Sunnyview's Buddy Jones, MH; GMHR Sunnyview's Special K, MH; GMHR, WR Sunnyview's Majestic Knight, MH; and GMHR, WR Sunnyview's Alaskan Black Sugar.

TAPNOD LABRADORS of Barking Heights Kennel was owned by Don and Patricia Ann Petrulis. This kennel, dating from 1971, was located in Tulsa, Oklahoma. Foundation stock included Ch. Chestnut Wrangler's Brandy, CD, WC and Ch. Wingmasters Cobc of Mandingo, CD,

WC. Other winners are Ch. Barking Heights Black Bury Jam; Ch. Sandbars Country Minny, CD; Ch. Barking Heights Nelly Dean; Ch. Barking Heights KoKo Krispie; and Ch. Could Be's Sure Man. Don Petrulis is well known at midwestern dog shows for being an outstanding photographer.

Judith S. Aycock established **TRUMARC KENNEL** in Sanger, Texas, in 1970. Her foundation stock was FC, AFC Trumarc's Raider and NFC, AFC Joaquin Honcho. Other winners carrying the kennel name are: Dual Ch. AFC Trumarc's Triple Threat; FC, NAFC Trumarc's Zip Code; FC, AFC Trumarc's Hot Pursuit; FC, AFC Trumarc's Ziparoo; and FC, AFC Trumarc's Sprinter.

Carroll Ann Lewandowski of East Aurora, New York, established her **VAN LEE KENNEL** in 1970. Her primary interest is fieldwork, as proven by the following winners: Van Lee's Daisy Mae, MH; Van Lee's TNT, SH; and Van Lee's Maximum Brew, JH.

VENETIAL LABRADORS kennel was founded in 1964 in Massapequa, New York, by Charlotte Veneziano. A leading chocolate sire for this kennel is Ch. Henning's Mills Master Blend. Winners under this kennel's banner are: Ch. Venetian Miss, Ch. Venetian's Snow Queen, Ch. Venetian Joyful Bridget, Ch. Venetian's Shababaland Hit Parade, Ch. Venetian's Mijan Drummer Boy, and Ch. Venetian's Blender de Chablais.

WA-LUKE RETRIEVERS was established in Mercer Island, Washington, in 1970 by Charles L. Hill. The leading stud at this field-trial kennel was the 1975 NFC, 1976 NAFC, 1976 CNFC, and 1977 CNFC, FC, AFC, and CFC Wanapum Darts Dandy.

WHYGIN KENNEL of Helen Ginnel dates from the 1940s. This kennel produced many winners that can be found in pedigrees of leading dogs today. These include Ch. Whygin Poppit, Ch. Whygin Skia, Ch. Whygin Campaign Promise, Ch. Whygin John Duck, Ch. Whygin The Bedford Brat, and Ch. Whygin Gold Bullion.

WINTERSET LABRADORS of Enid and Sel Bloome is located in Norwalk, Connecticut. Their breeding program is based on Ch. Killingworth's Valiant Lady, CD, and Killingworth Winterset My Jo, CD.

WORLD FAMOUS LABRADORS was established in Woodland, California, in 1972 by Sal Gelardi. Winners from this field-trial kennel include: AFC Chuk Chukar Chuk; AFC World Famous Sweet Pea; FC, AFC Chukar's Big Jake; FC, AFC T. T. Tucker; and FC, AFC Wild Hearted Dinah.

YARROW KENNEL of Bridgewater, Virginia, was founded in 1971 by Mrs. Beth Sweigart. In addition to Labrador Retrievers, Mrs. Sweigart also raised Airedales. Foundation Labrador Retriever stock is represented by Ch. Springfield's Ondine, CD, WC and the stud Ch. Poolstead Peer, who was co-owned with Mrs. R. V. Clark. Other winners were: Ch. Bravo's Pandora of Yarrow; Ch. Yarrow's The Magnus; Ch. Bravo's Liberated Lady; and Ch. Yarrow's Tango of Bravo, CD, later owned by Mrs. Jane Borders.

Ch. Highlands Ruffian, owned by G. Knobloch. Photo © John Ashbey.

chapter fifteen

LABRADOR RETRIEVERS IN OTHER COUNTRIES

The oldest kennel club in the world is the Kennel Club in England, with a founding date of 1873. The second oldest is the American Kennel Club, founded in 1884. In France, 1884 was also the year in which the Société d'Acclimation was formalized into the Société Centrale pour l'Amelioration des Races de Chiens. This title has more recently been shortened to Societe Centrale Canine.

Other early organizations were the New Zealand Kennel Club, 1886; the Kennel Club of Denmark (Dansk Kennelklub), 1887; the Kennel Club of Sweden (Svenska Kennel Klubben), 1888; the Canadian Kennel Club, 1888; and the Finnish Kennel Club (Suomen Kennelliitt-Finska Kennelklubben), 1889. More recent clubs are the German Kennel Club (Verband für das Deutsche Hundewesen); the Spanish Central Society (Real Sociedad Central Fomento de las Razas Caninas en España); the Portugûes Kennel Club (Clube Portuguese de Canicultura); and the Australian National Kennel Council, established as recently as 1958. This latter organization serves as a central unit for the clubs of the various states of Australia. The Scandinavian Kennel Union, founded in 1953, serves the same function for the four Scandinavian countries.

While the Kennel Club in England was not established until 1873, a group

Left to right: English Ch. Sandylands Busy Liz, English Ch. Sandylands Girl Friday, English Ch. Sandylands Mercy, English Ch. Sandylands Garry, English Ch. Sandylands Come Rain; English Ch. Sandylands Blaze, and English Ch. Sandylands Waghorn Honesty, owned by Mrs. Gwen Broadley and Mr. Garner Anthony of Sandylands Kennels. Thomas Fall Photography.

Left to right: English Ch. Sandlylands Midnight Magic, English Ch. Sandylands Storm-Along, English Ch. Sandylands Mark, and English Ch. Sandylands Newinn Columbus, owned by Mrs. Gwen Broadley and Mr. Garner Anthony of Sandylands Kennels. Thomas Fall Photography.

of interested breeders had more or less formalized a classification of dogs as early as 1859. Dogs were divided into two categories, Sporting and Non-Sporting. This division was formalized in 1881 and continued until 1947, when Sporting was further subdivided into Hounds, Gundogs, and Terriers. The present group divisions in England are somewhat similar to those in the United States: Hound, Gundog, Working, Terrier, Toy, and Utility. While these divisions may correspond between the two countries, the same dogs are not necessarily in the same groups in both countries. In England, the Shih Tzus are in the Utility Group instead of the Toy Group, and Schnauzers are also in the Utility Group instead of the Terrier and Working groups. Labrador Retrievers in England are classified as Gundogs.

In England, a championship is not based on a point system as it is in the United States. The winning of three Challenge Certificates (CCs) under three different judges entitles a dog to be called champion. The number of CCs to be awarded per year to any breed is based on the average registration per year over a three-year period. The allocation of CCs for Labrador Retrievers by the Kennel Club for 1996 and 1997 was thirty-nine sets with eleven of these going to the breed clubs and twenty-eight to the group and general championship shows. The maximum number of CCs for any breed is currently forty and the minimum is five where CCs are allocated to Crufts, the Scottish Kennel Club, the Welsh Kennel Club, the Birmingham Dog Show Society, and one breed club.

The Kennel Club in England divides the entries for both dogs and bitches into eight classes. They are: Special Puppy, for dogs six to nine months; Puppy, six to twelve months; Junior, six to eighteen months; Maiden, for dogs that have never won a first prize; Novice, for dogs that have not won a Challenge Certificate or more than three first prizes; Graduate, for dogs that have not won a Challenge Certificate or more than four first prizes; Open, for any dog; and Veteran, for dogs seven years or older. The Kennel Club sponsors both open and championship shows. Challenge Certificates are available only at championship shows. One of the interesting differences between judging in England and in the United States is the way in which the judges report on their assignments. Judges' comments are regularly published in the *English Dog World*. The judge discusses the strengths and weaknesses of dogs that he placed first and second at a show. His comments are public for all to see—both owner and competitor.

The German Kennel Club sponsors a World Championship Show. Breed winners here can earn, in a single show, the titles of German Champion and World Champion, and the Certificat d'Aptitude au Champion at Internationale (CACIB) award. Each dog is given one of the following five ratings: Excellent, Very Good, Good, Satisfactory, and Unsatisfactory.

France divides its 130 recognized breeds into 8 groups. The Germans divide their sixty-six breeds into five groups. Spain lists fifteen breeds divided into four groups.

ENGLAND

Total dog registrations in England rose from 11,650 in 1900 to 264,091 in 1995. The increase has been steady with the exception of the war years: 1910–18,918; 1920–16,189; 1930–48,784; 1940–13,968; 1950–100,433; 1960–133,618; 1970–175,074; 1980–201,620; 1990–270,769; and 2000–247,299. The number of breeds recognized by the Kennel Club of England is 154.

The registration figures in Table 15-1 indicate that while the Labrador Retriever is not as popular in England as he was several years ago, he still was ranked third among all breeds in 1975, which was the year that the Kennel Club decided to discontinue the compilation of individual breed statistics. In 1980, the club went back to the old system and once again is keeping records of individual breed registrations. The most popular breed in 2000 was the Labrador Retriever, with a registration of 34,888 dogs.

It would be impossible to name all of the kennels in England that have raised Labrador Retrievers over the years. The list is limited to those that have been the most active in recent years.

BLAIRCOURT KENNEL was established in Glasgow, Scotland, by Mrs. Marjorie Cairns. Carrying the Blaircourt prefix are: Ch. Ruler of Blaircourt, Ch. Tessa of Blaircourt, Ch. Wander of Blaircourt, Ch. Imp of Blaircourt, and Ch. Sandylands Tweed of Blaircourt. Am. Eng. Can. Ch. Sam of Blaircourt proved to be a significant stud dog for Labrador Retrievers in the United States.

SANDYLANDS KENNEL, in Daventry, Northants, has had a great influence on the breed, not only in England, but also in the United States, Australia, South Africa, and Scandinavia. Sandylands was established in 1930 by Mrs. Gwen Broadley and Mr. Garner Anthony. Mrs. Broadley is also an international judge.

English Ch. Timspring Little Iuc, owned by Mrs. Joan Macan of Timspring Kennels. Diane Pearce Photography.

English Ch. Timspring Sirius, owned by Mrs. Joan Macan of Timspring Kennels. Diane Pearce Photography.

English Shooting Ch. Lasgarn Ludovic, owned by E. G. and R. L . Edwards of Lasgarn Kennels. Anne Roslin-Williams Photography.

TABLE 15-1. LABRADOR RETRIEVER REGISTRATIONS IN ENGLAND

Year	Number	Rank
1985	15,156	2
1986	14,625	2
1987	13,914	2
1988	13,674	2
1989	26,392	1
1990	25,456	2
1991	24,978	1
1992	25,488	1
1993	25,261	1
1994	29,118	1
1995	32,429	1
1996	34,844	1
1997	34,778	1
1998	35,978	1
1999	33,398	1
2000	34,888	1

Shooting Ch. Nokeener May Blossom of Lasgarn, owned by E. G. and R. L. Edwards of Lasgarn Kennels. Anne Roslin-Williams Photography.

She has judged regularly in England, as well as in the United States and Australia. She has judged Best in Show at Crufts and at Santa Barbara.

The kennel has bred or owned more than sixty-five champions. Some of the winners from Sandylands are Ch. Sandylands Midnight Magic, Ch. Sandylands Come Rain, Ch. Sandylands Blaze, Ch. Sandylands Mark, and Ch. Sandylands Storm-Along.

E. R. and R. L. Edwards established their **LASGARN KENNEL** in Ponty Pool, Gwent, in 1950 to raise English Cocker Spaniels. Labrador Retrievers were added in 1963. Foundation Labrador Retriever stock came from Sandylands, Nokeener, and Ballyduff kennels. These crossbreedings produced winners such as Sh. Ch. Lasgarn Ludovic and Sh. Ch. Nokeener May Blosson of Lasgarn. (Sh. Ch. stands for Shooting Champion and is a field-certification championship title.)

TIMSPRING KENNEL was founded in 1961 by Mrs. Joan Macan in Berkhamsted, Hertfordshire. Sandylands and Ballyduff dogs served as foundation stock here also. Home-bred winners are Ch. Timspring Mace, Ch. Timspring Little Tuc, Ch. Timspring Jubilant, and Ch. Timspring Sirius. All of the kennel dogs are trained as gundogs.

Among the other leading English kennels and their owners are: POWHATAN LABRADOR RETRIEVERS, Major and Mrs. R. C. Aikenhead of Suffolk; POOLSTEAD LABRADOR RETRIEVERS, Mr. and Mrs. R. V. Hepworth of Cheshire; MANSERGH KENNEL, Mrs. Roslin Williams of Yorkshire; COLINWOOD LABRADOR RETRIEVERS, Mr. and Mrs. P. C. Woolf of Kent; MEADLANDS LABRADOR RETRIEVERS, Lindsey and Michael Wright of Essex; BRAEDUKE KENNEL, Major and Mrs. E. J. B. Wynyard of Northhampton; and BINGLEY KENNEL, Marjorie Booth of Yorkshire.

Canadian Ch. Runroy, owned by Tom and Phyllis Philip.

Canadian Ch. Kindsdale's Abracadabra, owned by Diane and Gordon MacMillan.

Additional current breeders include: CLASSICWAY LABRADOR RETRIEVERS, Daphne and Ernie Darby of Warwickshire; BRANDALE LABRADOR RETRIEVERS, Janice Poulsom of Yorkshire; FREDWELL KENNEL, Mrs. J. Wells-Meacham of Hertfordshire; KERLSTONE LABRADOR RETRIEVERS, Mr. and Mrs. W. Livingston of Ayrshire; and LIDDLY LABRADOR RETRIEVERS, H. A. Saunders of Newbury.

CANADA

The Labrador Retriever has been popular in Canada for many years both as a bench dog and as a field dog. The Canadian Kennel Club registration figures for 1995 indicate that the Labrador Retriever was the most popular dog for that year. Table 15-2 reflects registrations for the Labrador Retriever for the years 1990 to 2000.

A number of kennels in Canada have been active in the breeding and showing of Labrador Retrievers during the last thirty years. The following kennels have enjoyed success both as breeders and exhibitors.

Carole J. Nickerson established **CARHO KENNEL** in 1975 in Nova Scotia. Her first show dog was Ch. Wimberways Victory Rocket. The foundation

TABLE 15-2. CANADIAN LABRADOR RETRIEVER REGISTRATIONS

YEAR	TOTAL # DOGS
1990	6,873
1991	6,631
1992	6,919
1993	7,464
1994	8,719
1995	9,478
1996	9,018
1997	9,532
1998	10,140
1999	10,129
2000	9,336

bitch, Ch. Georgie Girl at Wimberway, produced Ch. Carho's Coffee Break, TT and Ch. Carho's Seminole Wind. The obedience area is represented by Carho's Seminole Vision, CD, with her owner Bill Dyer.

Ontario has been the home of **DEVONSLEIGH KENNEL** since 1988, when it was established by Joanne Fernall. Dogs representing this kennel are Glenacres Bailey Harbour, CD and Ch. Amaranth's Chevy Chase.

GHILLIE'S KENNEL was established by Mike and Maggie Guinn in 1968 in Calgary, Alberta. Their foundation stock was of English bloodlines through Ch. Halsinger Laddie and Ch. Ridgegreen Taffee Au Lait. Some two dozen champions carry the Ghillie prefix in their title These winners include Dual Ch. Ghillie's Nimpkish Sunshine, Ch. Ghillie's Windjammer, Ch. Ghillie's Sand Dollar, and Ch. Ghillie's Salt Water Taffee.

KINGSDALE KENNEL was founded by Diane and Gordon MacMillan in 1988 on Prince Edward Island. The foundation stud, Heldercrest Max of Kingsdale, was acquired in the United States. Dogs carrying this kennel prefix are Ch. Kingsdale's Bracken at Sandrok, Ch. Kingsdale's Goodtyme Charlie, Ch. Kingsdale's Lindenball Su Zee Q, and Ch. Kingsdale's Abracadabra.

Edward Boisclair of Quebec founded his **PINE GROVE KENNEL** in 1994. His foundation bitches, Soleidelaube Milady Bonnie and Soleidelaube Milady Capucine, are out of Ch. Ebonylane's Honnie.

Tom and Phyllis Phillip located their **RO-SHAN KENNEL** in Chrysler, Ontario, in 1965. Some thirty champion dogs carry the Ro-Shan prefix. Among them are: Ch. Ro-Shan's Run Happy Hopper, CD; Ch. Ro-Shan's Happy Shoe Chopper, CD; and Ch. Ro-Shan's Kristo Leaping Lisa.

SELAMAT KENNEL of Mrs. Dale Haines of Drumbo, Ontario, dates from 1968. Mrs. Haines started her breeding program primarily with field dogs of Sandylands and Castlemore bloodlines. Winners

Canadian Ch. Ro-Shan Fancy Cove Mo, owned by Tom and Phyllis Philip.

English Ch. Timspring Jubliant, owned by Joan Macan. Diane Pearce Photography.

AM. CAN. Ch. Triple L's Davey Crocket owned by Carl and Jan Liepmann.

at this kennel include: Ch. Castlemore Martin, CD, WC; Ch. Selamat's Chocolate Terra; Ch. Selamat's Cottonwood Hank; and Selamat's Midas Touch, UD.

WIMBERWAY KENNEL of Sandy Briggs has been located in Claremont, Ontario, since 1960. The foundation stock for Wimberway carried the Blyth and Briarley bloodlines and was principally of English breeding. More than 100 Canadian champions have been bred or owned by Wimberway Kennel. Many have also completed their titles in the United States and Bermuda. These dogs include the multiple Best-in-Show-winning Am. Can. Ber. Ch. Wimberway's Friendly Freddy, WC and his son Can. Ber. Ch. Wimberway's Cutty Sark, CD, WC, who was a Best-in Show winner. Others are Am. Can. Ch., Can. OTCh. Wimberway's Wateaki, WC, Am. CDX; Ch. Wimberway's Everway, CDX; Am. Can. Ch. Wimberway's Odin, CD; and Can. Ber. Ch. Wimberway the Beguiling Spirit, Can. Ber. CD.

LABRADOR RETRIEVER HALL OF FAME

This section is presented to make available to Labrador Retriever breeders and exhibitors an opportunity to study pictures and pedigrees of some of the dogs that have been winning in the showring and in fieldtrial competition during the last twenty-five years. While pictures occasionally appear in magazines, they usually are not accompanied by pedigrees, which means that little or no evaluation can be made of the breeding program that produced a particular dog. Breeders will have an opportunity to study various bloodlines and to compare specimens of these lines. The dogs are listed in alphabetical order to facilitate reference to a particular animal.

By studying the pedigrees, you will note that many of these winners are closely line-bred, and in some cases they are even inbred. There are also examples of outcrosses.

The dogs presented here are representatives from most parts of the United States, Canada, and England. The leading breeding lines are also represented. Some of the dogs are from the past, and some are just beginning their show or field careers.

Ch. Heartlands East Hill Amanda, owned by Sandy McCabe. Photo © Downey Dog Show Photography.

DUAL CH. GRANGEMEAD PRECOCIOUS
FC FREEHAVEN MUSCLES
Grangemead Sharon
FC & AFC PAHA SAPA CHIEF II
FC & AFC THE SPIDER OF KINGSWERE
Treasure State Be-Wise
FC DEER CREEL BE-WISE
NFC & NAFC SUPER CHIEF
DUAL CH. GRANGEMEAD PRECOCIOUS
DUAL CH. CHEROKEE BUCK
Grangemead Sharon
Ironwood Cherokee Chica
NFC & NAFC CORK OF OAKWOOD LANE
Glen Water Fantom
Little Peggy Black Gum
NFC & NAFC AIR EXPRESS
Huron's Black Prince
Sambo of Somonnauk II
Duchess of Stonegate
Nettley Creeks Sugar
DUAL CH. BRACKEN SWEEP
Nelgard's Madam Queen
FC LADY'S DAY AT DEER CREEK
CAN. DUAL CH. DART OF NETTLEY CREEK
NFC MARVADEL BLACK GUM
Stonegate's Brazen Beau
Camay Classy Chassis
Stonegates Susie
DUAL CH. MATCHMAKER FOR DEER CREEK
Lucky Linda of Stonegate
Stonegate Char

August and Louise Belmont

NFC and AFC Air Express

Ch. Ashridge Robin Hood. Bernard Kernan Photography.

ENG. CH. SANDYLANDS MARK
ENG. CH. BALLYDUFF MARKETEER
ENG. CH. BALLYDUFF MARINA
ENG. CH. SQUIRE OF BALLYDUFF
Eduny Sandpiper
Sparkle of Tuddenham
Bridget of Tuddenham and Ballyduff
CH. KUPROS SPARTACUS
ENG. CH. KEYSUN TEKO OF BLONDELLA
ENG. SH. CH. NEWINN KESTREL
Newinn Fleur
Kupros Kirsch
ENG. CH. SANDYLANDS MARK
Ballyduff Morella
ENG. CH. BALLYDUFF MARINA
CH. ASHRIDGE ROBIN HOOD
ENG. CH. RULER OF BLAIRCOURT
ENG. CH. WANDERER OF BLAIRCOURT
Snipe of Luscander
Fredwell Never Say Die of Blaircourt
Sandylands Trust of Blaircourt
Gorse of Blaircourt
ENG. SH. CH. TESSA OF BLAIRCOURT
Fredwell Bridget
Powhatan Solo
Ballyduff Powhatan Gale
Powhatan Pearl
Fredwell Croquet
ENG. CH. BALLYDUFF HOLLYBRANCH KEITHRAY
Fredwell Ballyduff Cynthia
Pebblestreet Cindy

Carol A. Baugh
Ashridge Kennels

ENG.CH. KUPROS MASTER MARINER
ENG. CH. SANDYLANDS MY GUY
Sandylands Bramble
ENG. SH. CH. SANDYLANDS GADABOUT
ENG. CH. TRENOW BRIGADIER
Sandylands Rae
CH. LENCHES GALLIVANT
NZ SH. CH. CARPENNY CHATEAU CRANSPIRE
ENG. SH. CH. TIBBLESTONE THE CHORISTER
Sandylands Forever Amber at Tibblestone
Lenches Tiptop
Poolstead Pearl Bailey
Lenches Personality
Lenches Peppermint
CH. BORADORS BY GEORGE
CH. CHAFERN COURT STAR OF FABRACKEN
CH. HENNINGS MILL CRUSO
Lindall Miss Holly
CH. HUNT CLUB HENNINGS MILL GINO
Jayncourt Razzle Dazzle
Hennings Mills Country Charm
CH. COUNTRY PLACE O'HENNINGS MILL
CH. DEER RUNS SWEET CARAMEL CREAM
CH. ELYSIUM'S CITIZEN KANE
CH. BORADOR'S THE GOBLIN
Winterset Legendwood OP III
CH. BORADOR'S SWEET CHARITY
CH. DICKENDALL'S RAZZLE DAZZLE
Borador's Edgewater Harlow
Borador's Edgewater Echo

Vicky Creamer and Sally Bell

Ch. Boradors By George. Photo by Baines.

Ch. Cameo's Great Expectations.

Cranspire Skytrain
CH. RECEIVER OF CRANSPIRE
Pollys Pride of Genisval
CH. DICKENDALL RUFFY SH
CH. EIREANNACH BLACK COACHMAN
CH. MOORWOOD JEWEL
CH. BEAVER'S LAVINIA OF MOORWOOD
CH. DICKENDALL ARNOLD
CH. ALLEGHENY'S ECLIPSE
CH. MARSHLAND BLITZ
CH. MARSHLAND PAISLEY BROONE
Dickendalls A-Ha
CH. BRIARY BRACKEN
Dickendalls Rose Royce
Rasin Cain of Woodbrook CK
CH. CAMEO'S GREAT EXPECTATIONS
CH. MONARCH'S BLACK ARROGANCE
CH. BORADORS RIDGWAY REFLECTION
Ambleside Maraschino CD
CH. BORADORSS MCKENNA XEND CD
CH. COAL CREEKS BRIARY BREAKTHRU
CH. SIMERDOWN'S MCKENNA KENDELL CD
CH. MANDIGO'S SIMERDOWN DESTINY
CH. RIVERLANE'S OLYMPIC PRIDE
CH. MONARCH'S BLACK ARROGANCE
CH. SAILIN CAJUN'S CASANOVA CD
CH. ELYSIUM'S SAILIN CAT BALLOW
CH. DAYLIGHT REVERLANE'S GMEN CD
CH. SOMMERSETT GAMBLER
CH. DAYLIGHT SISSY GAMBLER
CH. DAYLIGHT'S BLACKTHORN SHEENA CD

Michael W. Baldree

CH. LOCKERBIE BLACKFELLA
Lockerbie Panda
    CH. ZELSTONE KATE
CH. LOCKERBIE KISMET
    CH. SANDYLANDS TWEED OF BLAIRCOURT
Lockerbie Sandylands Tidy
Sandylands Shadow
CH. LOCKERBIE BRIAN BORU, W.C.
    CH. SANDYLANDS TWEED OF BLAIRCOURT
CH. LOCKERBIE SANDYLANDS TARQUIN
Sandylands Shadow
Lockerbie Tackety Boots
    CH. RENACRE MALLARDHURN THUNDER
CH. LOCKERBIE PEBBLESTREET DINAH
Poolstead Polly Flinders
AM. & CAN. CH. CAMPBELLCROFT'S ANGUS, C.D., W.C.
    CH. LOCKERBIE KISMET
CH. LOCKERBIE BRIAN BORU, W.C.
Lockerbie Tackety Boots
CH. BRIARY'S TRACE OF BRIAN, C.D., W.C.
    CH. LOCKERBIE SANDYLANDS TARQUIN
CH. LOCKERBIE SHILLELAGH
Princess of Marlow
CH. CAMPBELLCROFT'S PEDE, C.D., W.C.
    CH. LOCKERBIE GOLDENTONE JENSEN
CH. SPENROCK'S CARDIGAN BAY
    AM., CAN. & BDA. CH. SPENROCK'S BANNER, W.C.
CH. AGBER DAISY OF CAMPBELLCROFT, C.D., W.C.
Whiskey Creek's Tween Bairn
CH. WHISKEY CREEK'S LISA
Brandy of Hamlin

Donald and Virginia Campbell
Campbellcroft Kennels

American and Canadian Ch. Campbellcroft's Angus, C.D., W.C. Fox and Cook Photography.

FC & NAFC Candlewoods Rambin Man.

NAFC NFC SUPER CHIEF
FA AFC AIR EXPRESS
    CH. DART OF NETLEY CREEDD
FC AFC ITCHIN' TO GO
Spring Frams Lucky
Still Water Peggy
Toni of Wanapum
FC AFC WILDERNESS HARLEY TO GO
    NFC CNFC RIVER OAKS CORKY
NFC FC RIVER OAKS RASCAL
Random Rapscallion
AFC BLACK GOLD'S CANDLEWOOD KATE
    AFC NFC SYOER CHIEF
FC AFC CANDLEWOODS NELLIE B GOOD
Gahonk's Rebel Queen
FC NAFC CANDLEWOODS RAMBIN MAN
    FC AFC TRUMARC'S RAIDER
NFC AFC SAN JOAQUIN HONCHO
Doxie Gyypsy Taurus
NFC NAFC CANDLEWOODS SUPER TANKER
    NFC FC RIVER OAKS RASCAL
Candlewoods Delta Dash
    FC AFC CANDLEWOODS NELLIE B GOOD
Tanks Candlewood Kate
    FC AFC CFC TRIEVEN THUNDERHEADD
AFC FC CFC BIG RIVER DAGO
Big River Mancy
Rainbow's Garbo Inkling
    NFC FC RIVER OAKD RASCAL
Garbo Ink
Little Miss Mischief

Jim Powers

CH. WHYGIN GOLD BULLION
CH. SHAMROCK ACRES CASEY
CH. WHYGIN GENTLE JULIA OF AVEC
CH. SHAMROCK ACRES LIGHT BRIGADE
CH. WHYGIN POPPITT
CH WHYGIN BUSY BELINDA
Bengali Sari
AM. CAN. CH. FRANKLINS GOLDEN MANDINGO CD, WCX
CH. KINLEY COMET OF HARHAM
CH. FRANKLINS SUN STAR
CH. SUNSET ROAD OF FRANKLIN
CH. FRANKLINS TALLY OF BURYWOOD
CH. JASPER OF ELMONA
CH. FRANKLINS SPRING DAWN
CH. VELVET LASSIE OF FRANKLIN
CH. CHARISMA'S LONE STAR RICK
CH. LOCKERBIE KISMET
CH. LOCKERBIE BRIAN BORU
Lockerbie Tackety Boots
CH. WILDWING'S MCDUFF
CH. SHAMROCK ACRES LIGHT BRIGADE
Shamrock Acres Spring Fever
CH. SHAMROCK ACRES ONE WAY TICKET
Tanglewood Sassy Celina WC
CH. SHAMROCK ACRES LIGHT BRIGADE
CH. SHAMROCK ACRES GOLDENROD
CH. WHYGIN GENTLE JULIA OF AVEC
AM. CAN. CH. WRENWELL'S WHINSTONE
CH. SHAMROCK ACRES DONNYBROOK
AM. CAN. CH. SHAMROCK ACRES REFLECTION
CH. SHAMROCK ACRES EARLY BIRD

Joyce and Roy Loyless

Ch. Charisma's Lone Star Rick.

Ch. Chestnut Wrangler's Brandy. Don Petrulis Photography.

CH. INDIAN VALLEY ROB ROY
CH. COULD BE'S HAVEN ROCK
CH. COULD BE'S MISS ERABLE
CH. COULD BE'S RUSTY ROCK
Nelgard's Captain Stuart
CH. BEER'S MUG, C.D.
Joydale's Black Popwder
CH. COULD BE'S CHESTNUT WRANGLER
Bart of Blaircourt
CH. INDIAN VALLEY ROB ROY
Altiora of Blaircourt
CH. COULD BE'S HANDFUL
CH. MIGHTY MANFRED OF MARYGLO, C.D.
CH. COULD BE'S MISS ERABLE
CH. BEER'S MUG, C.D.
CH. CHESTNUT WRANGLER'S BRANDY, C.D.
Bart of Blaircourt
CH. INDIAN VALLEY ROB ROY
Altiora of Blaircourt
CH. COULD BE'S HAVEN ROCK
CH. MIGHTY MANFRED OF MARYGLO, C.D.
CH. COULD BE'S MISS ERABLE
CH. BEER'S MUG, C.D.
Could Be's Cola Color
NFC & AFC SUPER CHIEF
Shamrock Acres Could Be Super
CH. COULD BE'S MISS ERABLE
Kit of Warwick
CH. COULD BE'S HAVEN ROCK
Gemini Rock
Could Be's Mistifier

Don and Pat Petrulis
Tapnod's Labradors

Lockerbie Panda
  CH. LOCKERBIE KISMET
    Lockerbie Sandylands Tidy
CH. LOCKERBIE BRIAN BORU, S.C.
    CH. LOCKERBIE SANDYLANDS TARQUIN
  Lockerbie Tackety Boots
    CH. LOCKERBIE PEBBLESTREET DINAH
AM. & CAN. CH. COALCREEK'S BRIARY BREAKTHRU
    CH. LOCKERBIE STANWOOD GRANADA
  CH. SPENROCK ANTHONY ADVERSE
    AM., CAN. & BDA. CH. SPENROCK'S BANNER
Briary Allegra
    CH. LOCKERBIE BRIAN BORU, W.C.
  CH. BRIARY FLORADORA
    Follytower Cressida
CH. COALCREEK'S GIMME A BREAK
    ENG. CH. SANDYLANDS TWEED OF BLAIRCOURT
  Whiskey Creek Tweed's Bairn
    Ramah Roman Hostess
CH. SCRIMSHAW ANOTHER DEACON
    Chebacco Walter R.
  Scrimshaw Mother Carey
    Jointe Scrimshaw O'Spindrift
CH. SCRIMSHAW MY SIN
    CH. SANDYLANDS SHOWMAN OF LANDROW
  Cliveruth Harvester
    Cliveruth Wendover Joanna
CH. SANDYLANDS CRYSTAL
    ENG. CH. WISHWOOD WINSTON
  Cliveruth Sandylands Witch
    Sandylands Tammy

George and Lillian Knobloch
Highland Kennels

Ch. Coalcreek's Gimme A Break owned by George and Lillian Knobloch. Photo © Alverson Photographers.

Ch. Dark Star of Franklin.

    CH. RAFFLES OF EARLSMOOR
  CH. & FC SHED OF ARDEN
    FC DECOY OF ARDEN
Labcroft Game Boy
    FC GUN OF ARDEN
  Mueller's Judy
    Duchess of Hickory Hurst
CH. LABCROFT MISTER CHIPS
    Oldbridge Bob
  Chief of Oldbridge
    Glenravel Tryst
Labcroft North Wind
    L'ile Larry
  Black Meg of Avandale
    Meg of Greeymar
AM. & CAN. CH. DARK STAR OF FRANKLIN
    CH. RAFFLES OF EARLSMOOR
  CH. & FC SHED OF ARDEN
    FC DECOY OF ARDEN
FC PICKPOCKET FOR DEER CREEK
    CH. BANCHORY TRUMP OF WINGAN
  Peggy of Pheasant Lawn
    Laquer
CH PITCH OF FRANKLIN
    CH. RAFFLES OF EARLSMOOR
  CH EARLSMOOR MOOR OF ARDEN
    FC DECOY OF ARDEN
Wardwyn Warbler
    Fife of Kennoway
  CH. BUDDHA OF ARDEN
    Pitch of Arden

Mr. & Mrs. B. W. Ziessow

CH. MANSERGE MOOSE
CH. EIREANLACH BLACK COACHMAN
Powttatass Sable
CH. ALLEGHENY'S ECLIPSE
CH. SANDYLANDS MACK
CH. ALLEGHENY'S BEZIQUE
Ellerthwaite Jay
CH. MARSHLAND BLITZ
Sandylands Stormey Weather
CH. ELSIUM'S THUNDERSTORM
Briary Banbury Belle
CH. MARSHLAND PAISLEY BROOME
Ardmargha Samson
Hawkett Paisley Amber Breeze
CH. PAISLEY'S APRICOT DELIGHT
CH. DELIGHT HEIR OF ELENDIL
Cambremer Petrocelli
Cranspire Sky Train
Poolstead Purpose of Cangaire
AM. & ENGL. SH. CH. RECCILYS OF CRANSPIRE
SH. CH. ALEWINN KERSTAL
Pollly Pride of Genistal
Heatherbourne Genistal
CH. DELIGHT CREME DE MENTHE
CH. SANDYLANDS MACKWELL OF LOCKERBIE
CH. NORTHWOOD SANDMAN
CH. FINCHINFIELD FANTASIA
CH. AQUARIUS PARR'S DELIGHT
CH. SUNNYBROOK ACRES SANDPIPER
CH. SUNNYBROOK ACRES SOUNDER
CH. SUNNYBROOK ACRES BLACK GOLD

Sharon Parr
Delight Labradors

Ch. Delight Heir of Elendil.

Ch. East Hill Sumo Safari Thyme. Alex Smith Photography.

Kelleygreen's Pug
CH. KELLEYGREEN'S SIR LANCELOT
Stajantor's Bridget
CH. STEPAMGAR'S MASAI MARA SIMBA WC JH CD
CH. PINE VALLEY C & L BUBBA
Pine Valley Majestic's Dawn
Welcove Pine Valley Chipewa
AM. CAN. CH. SUMO'S SIMEN KARIBU KENYA
CH. DICKENDALL RUFFY JH
CH. BROAD REACH BOCEPHUS SH
CH. BROAD REACH MOTEE JH
Sumo's Merci Bo-Coup
Hennwood's Mrembo Rafiki
Sumo's Poppyfield Arrogance
Poppyfield's True Arroganc
AM. CAN. CH. EAST HILL SUMO SAFARI THYME
AM. CAN. CH. ROCKYACRES SULTAN OF AYR
CAN. CH. KERRYMARK BALLAD OF CORHAMPTON
AM. CAN. CH. LOBUFF'S SUNDOWN AT KERRYMA
AM. CAN. CH. CORHAMPTON'S BARLEY O'BRADY
AM. CAN. CH. EBONYLANE'S ASIAN
CAN. CH. EBONYLANE'S UPTOWN GIRL
CAN. CH. EBONYLANE'S FORTUNE TELLER
AM. CAN. CH. ASHSTONE EASTHILL STEP'S THYME
Briary Bonfire of Windsong
Corhampton's Mr. Jojo Bojangles
CAN. CH. AMARANTH'S SAUCY SARAH CD
CAN. CH. CORHAMPTON'S VICTORIAN LACE
CAN. CH. AMARANTH'S SPELLBOUNDER CD
CAN. CH. CORHAMPTON'S SUNSHINE
CAN. CH. LINDERHALL'S MY DEAR ABBY

Paul Pobega

CH. LOCKERBIE KISMET
    CH. LOCKERBIE BRIAN BORU, W.C.
    Lockerbie Tackety Boots
CH. WILDWING MC DUFF
    CH. SHAMROCK ACRES LIGHT BRIGADE
    Shamrock Acres Spring Fever
    CH. SHAMROCK ACRES ONE WAY TICKET
CH. ELYOD'S MACBETH OF CANTERBURY
    NFC MARTEN'S LITTLE SMOKEY
    CH. SHAMROCK ACRES EBONY LANCER
    CH. WHYGIN GENTLE JULIA OF AVEC
Elyod's Ebylu Eggenshire
    Glenkarnock's Fancy Dan
    CH. ELYOD'S LEWISTON LULU
    CH. MISS PEGGY PONDWEED
CH. ELDEN'S TIGGER TOO
    CH. LOCKERBIE BRIAN BORU, W.C.
    CH. BARNABY'S O'BRIAN, C.D.
    Firsty Fresca
CH. BARNABY'S APOLLO REBELLION
    CH. SHAMROCK ACRES SHADOW BOXER
    Siridan Electric Spark
    CH. DON HEAD GINA'S MISCHIEF
CH. APPOLLO'S SILVERMIST
    CH. SHAMROCK ACRES LIGHT BRIGADE
    CH. JACKSON OF GREENLANE
    CH. BAROKE'S QUEEN OF SPADES
Wildwing's Penny Ante
    CH. SHAMROCK ACRES LIGHT BRIGADE
    Shamrock Acres Spring Fever
    CH. SHAMROCK ACRE ONE WAY TICKET

Elden Williams
Elden's Labrador Retrievers

Ch. Elden's Tigger Too.

Ch. Elyod's MacBeth of Canterbury. Carl Lindemaier Photography.

Lockerbie Panda
CH. LOCKERBIE KISMET
    Lockerbie Sandylands Tidy
CH. LOCKERBIE BRIAN BORU, W.C.
    CH. SANDYLANDS TARQUIN
    Lockerbie Tackety Boots
    CH. LOCKERBIE PEBBLESTREET DINAH
CH. WILDWING'S MC DUFF
    CH. SHAMROCK ACRES CASEY JONES, C.D.
    CH. SHAMROCK ACRES LIGHT BRIGADE
    CH. WHYGIN BUSY BELINDA
Shamrock Acres Spring Fever
    CH. WHYGIN ROYAL ROCKET
    CH. SHAMROCK ACRES ONE WAY TICKET
    CH. WHYGIN CAMPAIGN PROMISE
AM. & CAN. CH. ELYOD'S MACBETH OF CANTERBURY
    FC CROWDER
    NFC MARTEN'S LITTLE SMOKEY
    FC MARTEN'S LITTLE BULLET
    CH. SHAMROCK ACRES EBONY LANCER
    CH. WHYGIN GOLD BULLION
    CH. WHYGIN GENTLE JULIA OF AVEC
    Whygin Black Gambit of Avec
Elyod's Ebylu Eggenshire
    NFC DEL TONE COLVIN
    Glenkarnock's Fancy Dan
    Glengarvin's Black Bess
CH. ELYOD'S LEWISTON LULU
    AM. & CAN. FC SALT VALLEY OTTIE
    CH. MISS PEGGY PONDWEED
    Chonna's Black Diamond

Elden Williams
Elden's Labrador Retrievers

ENG. CH. SANDYLANDS TANDY
   CH. CAREFREE OF KIETHRAY
      ENG. CH. HOLLYBEAUT OF KIETHRAY
Grovetons Koko Khalif
      AM. & Eng. CH. KIMVALLEY CRISPIN
   Grovetons Affable Andora
      Lady Tinkerbelle of Groveton
CH. HIGHLANDS BRONZE CHIEFTAIN
      CH. LOCKERBIE SANDYLANDS TARQUIN
   CH. GROVETONS COPPER BUCK SHOT
      Lady Tinkerbelle of Groveton
Highlands Egyptian Queen
      Black Ho-Beau's Ditto
   Sambeau's Cam
      Samantha's Secret
AM. & CAN. CH. HIGHLANDS CHIVAS REGAL
      ENG. CH. SANDYLANDS TANDY
   ENG. CH. FOLLYTOWER MERRYBROOK BLACK STORM
      Follytower Old Black Magic
AM. & ENG. CH. LAWNWOODS HOT CHOCOLATE
      ENG. CH. LAWNWOODS FAME AND FORTUNE
   Lawnwoods Tapestry
      ENG. CH. POOLSTEAD PERSONALITY LAWNWOOD
Windshire Princess of Bree
      CH. CAREFREE OF KEITHRAY
   Grovetons Koko Khalif
      Grovetons Affable Andora
Grovetons Rambunctious
      CH. LOCKERBIE SANDYLANDS TARQUIN
   Grovetons Copper Penny
      Lady Tinkerbelle of Groveton

George and Lillian Knobloch
Highland Kennels

AM/CAN Ch. Highlands Chivas Regal, owned by G. Knobloch. Photo © Ashbey Photography.

Ch. Highlands Space Ranger was the No. 1 Labrador Retriever Breed System, 1995. Owned by George and Lillian Knobloch. © JC Photo.

CH. LOCKERBIE KISMET
   CH. LOCKERBIE BRIAN BORU, W.C.
      Lockerbie Tackety Boots
AM. & CAN. CH. COALCREEK'S BRIARY BREAKTHRU
      CH. SPENROCK ANTHONY ADVERSE
   Briary Allegra
      CH. BRIARY FLORADORA
CH. COALCREEK'S GIMME A BREAK
      Whiskey Creek Tweed's Bairn
   CH. SCRIMSHAW ANOTHER DEACON
      Scrimshaw Mother Carey
CH. SCRIMSHAW MY SIN
      Cliveruth Harvester
   CH. SANDYLANDS CRYSTAL
      Cliveruth Sandylands Witch
CH. HIGHLANDS SPACE RANGER
      AM & CAN CH. COALCREEKS BRIARY
   CH. COALCREEK'S GIMME A BREAK
      CH. SCRIMSHAW MY SIN
CH. HIGHLAND'S HONEY DIPPER
      CH. BROYHILL HENNINGS CASINO
   Hennings Mill's Bixby Kate
      CH. HENNINGS MILL IVORY CARGO
Highlands Sugar of Lake Pine
      AM. & CAN. CH. MONARCH'S BLACK ARROGANCE
   CH. DAVEOG SILKY BEAU
      Briary Marzipan
Spenrock Widgeon
      CH. SPENROCK TWEED OF WINFIELDS
   Spenrock Sopwith Pup
      Ludie II

George and Lillian Knobloch
Highland Kennels

Stonegates Captain
CFC, AFC, & FC YANKEE CLIPPER OF REO RAJ
Little Peggy Black Gum
FC & AFC MY REBEL
AFC DUKE OF ASHTON
Duchess of Miller
Prana's Replica of Bingo
Gahonk's Pow Wow
Cock of Oakwood Lane
CFC ACE HI ROYAL FLUSH
Queen Ace
Canvasback Dee
CFC BAKERS FERRY
Duxbak Dandy
Cornmoney Moria
1979 & 1980 NAFC & FC LAWHORN'S CADILLAC MACK
FC FREEHAVEN'S MUSCLES
FC & AFC PAHA SAPA CHIEF II
Treasurer State Be Wise
Spring Farms Lucky
DUAL CH. CHEROKEE BUCK
Ironwood Cherokee Chica
Glenwater Fantom
Creigh's Kalamity Kate of Brio
FC LARRY'S LASSEER
FC LARRY'S CAPTAIN HOOK
Ripco's Lady Jo
Madcap Imp of Brio
DUAL CH. RIDGEWOOD PLAYBOY
J.D.'s Shadee Playgirl
FC & AFC GRADY'S SHADEE LADY

Dennis Bath and Gerald Lawhorn

1979 and 1980 NAFC and FC Lawhorn's Cadillac Mack.

Ch. Lockerbie Brian Boru, W.C.

Ballyduff Treesholme Terryboy
CH. LOCKERBIE BLACKFELLA
CH. BALLYDUFF CANDY
Lockerbie Panda
Baredrop Bruce
CH. ZELSTONE KATE
FC ZELSTONE DARTER
CH. LOCKERBIE KISMET
CH. RULER OF BLAIRCOURT
ENG. CH. SANDYLANDS TWEED OF BLAIRCOURT
SH. CH. TESSA OF BLAIRCOURT
Lockerbie Sandylands Tidy
INT. CH. SAM OF BLAIRCOURT
Sandylands Shadow
Diant Pride
CH. LOCKERBIE BRIAN BORU, W.C.
CH. RULER OF BLAIRCOURT
ENG. CH. SANDYLANDS TWEED OF BLAIRCOURT
SH. CH. TESSA OF BLAIRCOURT
CH. LOCKERBIE SANDYLANDS TARQUIN
INT. CH. SAM OF BLAIRCOURT
Sandylands Shadow
Diant Pride
Lockerbie Tackety Boots
ENG. CH. SANDYLANDS TWEED OF BLAIRCOURT
CH. RENACRE MALLARDHURN THUNDER
Mallardhurn Pat
CH. LOCKERBIE PEBBLESTREET DINAH
CH. RENACRE MALLARDHURN THUNDER
Poolstead Polly Flinders
Braeduke Julia of Poolside

Ceylon and Marjorie Brainard
Briary Kennels

Thatch of Whitmore
CH. RAFFLES OF EARLSMOOR
Task of Whitmore
CH. & FC SHED OF ARDEN
Odds On
FC DECOY OF ARDEN
Peggy of Shipton
FC PICKPOCKET FOR DEER CREEK
Blenheim Scamp
CH. BANCHORY TRUMP OF WINGAN
Lady Daphnee
Peggy of Pheasant Lawn
FC BANCHORY VARNISH OF WINGAN
Laquer
Cheverella Dina
CH. PITCH OF FRANKLIN
Thatch of Whitmore
CH. RAFFLES OF EARLSMOOR
Task of Whitmore
CH. EARLSMORE MOOR OF ARDEN
Odds On
FC DECOY OF ARDEN
Peggy of Shipton
Wardwyn Warblen
Jericho Paul
Fife of Kennoway
Judy of Kennoway
CH BUDDHA OF ARDEN
Hiwood Risk
Pitch of Arden
Peggy of Shipton

Mrs. B. W. Ziessow

Ch. Pitch of Franklin.

Ch. Star's Sailerman of Seasac, C.D.X., W.C.

Lockerbie Panda
CH. LOCKERBIE KISMET
Lockerbie Sandylands Tidy
CH. LOCKERBIE BRIAN BORU, W.C.
CH. LOCKERBIE SANDYLANDS TARQUIN
Lockerbie Tackety Boots
CH. LOCKERBIE PEBBLESTREET DINAH
CH. ROSE'S EASTER STAR
FC & AFC CROOK'S TABOO PAT
Crook's El Torro
Black Rapids of Barranof
Winroc Wily Witch
DUAL CH. MARTEN'S LITTLE SMOKEY
Shamrock Acres P.D.Q.
CH. WHYGIN GENTLE JULIA OF AVEC
CH. STAR'S SAILERMAN OF SEASAC, C.D.X., W.C.
CH. SHAMROCK ACRES SNOW OF WHYGIN
Siridan Ponding Hail
CH. DON HEAD GINA'S MISCHIEF
Bairs Yellow Bull of Siridan
CH. FRANKLIN SUN STAR
Coll-A-Dene's Snowflake
Shamrock Acres Snowflake
AM. & CAN. CH. FREEMAN'S YELLOW QUEEN OF BULL
CH. SHAMROCK ACES LIGHT BRIGADE
Royal Oaks Jet
CH. SHAMROCK ACRES ROYAL OAKS, C.D.
Shannon Corbell of Blue Slide
Travis of Minniwawa
Ginger of Mariposa
Sierra Golden Honey

Art and Beth Davis
Sailin Labradors

Poppleton Beech Flight
CH. KINLEY MATADOR
Kinley Sparrowhawk
CH. KINLEY YORKSHIREMAN
CH. WHATSTANDWELL CORONET
Kinley Mantilla
CH. KINLEY CHARM
CH. SUDROK'S SPORT OF THUNDERBAY
CH. RULER OF BLAIRCOURT
CH. SANDYLANDS TWEED OF BLAIRCOURT
CH. TESSA OF BLAIRCOURT
CH. HOLLYBERRY OF KEITHRAY
Bickerton Salmon Prince
CH. HOLLYBANK BEAUTY
Ckookridge Gay Princess
CH. SUDROK'S DON POLO, U.D.
CH. RULER OF BLAIRCOURT
CH. SANDYLANDS TWEED OF BLAIRCOURT
CH. TESSA OF BLAIRCOURT
CH. SPORT OF SUNNYCREST
CH. KINLEY MATADOR
CH. MISS BLUE QUILL
Rhona of Blaircourt
Sudrok's Princess Pat
Bud's Pal O'Mine King
CH. STEVES GOLDEN REIGN
Wright's Golden Jill
CH. SUDROK MISS LIBERTY
Last Chance Shed
Last Chance Spice Queen
Last Chance Duchess

Jim Falkner

Ch. Sudrok's Don Polo, C.D.X., U.D.

Ch. Sunnybrook Acres Ace O'Spades. Photo by Noel.

AM. & CAN CH. SHAMROCK ACRES SONIC BOOM
CH. SHAMROCK ACRES DARK CLOUD
AM. & CAN. CH. WHYGIN CAMPAIGN PROMISE
CH. SHAMROCK ACRES FRINGE BENEFIT
CH. SHAMROCK ACRES LIGHT BRIGADE
Shamrock Acres Lollipop
CH. WHYGIN GENTLE JULIA OF AVEC
AM. & CAN. CH. SHAMROCK ACRES EBONYLANDE ACE, C.D.X.,W.C.
CH. SHAMROCK ACRES CASEY JONES, C.D.
CH. SHAMROCK ACRES LIGHT BRIGADE
CH. WHYGIN BUSY BELINDA
CH. SHAMROCK ACRES PEG OF MY HEART
AM. & CAN. CH. SHAMROCK ACRES SONIC BOOM
CH. SHAMROCK ACRES TWIGGY
AM. & CAN. CH. WHYGIN CAMPAIGN PROMISE
AM., CAN., BDA., BAH., VEZ., S. AM. & DOM CH. SUNNYBROOK ACRES
ACE O'SPADES, DOM., CAN. C.D.; P.R., VEZ., BDA., CDX; BDA. T.D.;
BAH. U.D.; AM. U.D.T.X., W.C.
Shamrock Acres Moonlighter
Could Be's Walk Like a Lion
CH. COULD BE'S BLACK ANGUS HEIFER
CH. SUNNYBROOK ACRES SANDPIPER
CH. SHAMROCK ACRES LIGHT BRIGADE
CH. SHAMROCK ACRES GOLDEN ACCENT
Shamrock Acres Kiss Me Kate
CH. SUNNYBROOK ACRES RAY'S HONEY, U.D., W.C.
CH. SHAMROCK ACRES CASEY JONES, C.D.
CH. SHAMROCK ACRES LIGHT BRIGADE
CH. WHYGIN BUSY BELINDA
CH. SUNNYBROOK ACRES BLACK GOLD
CH. COULD BE'S BLACK ANGUS
CH. COULD BE'S BLACK ANGUS HEIFER
Moore's Midnight Dream

Dr. and Mrs. John Ippensen
Sunnybrook Acres Kennel

CH. WHYGIN GOLD BULLION
AM. & CAN. CH. SHAMROCK ACRES SONIC BOOM
CH. WHYGIN GENTLE JULIA OF AVEC
Shamrock Acres Moonlight
AM. & CAN. CH. WHYGIN ROYAL ROCKET, C.D.
CH. SHAMROCK ACRES ONE WAY TICKET
AM. & CAN. CH. WHYGIN CAMPAIGN PROMISE
CH. COULD BE'S HARVEST MOON
AM. & CAN. CH. SHAMROCK SONIC BOOM
CH. COULD BE'S BLACK ANGUS
CH. GARMERETTE OF CHARLORU
CH. COULD BE'S BLACK ANGUS HEIFER
Could Be's Blade
Moore's Midnight Dream
Could Be's Mistifier
CH. SUNNYBROOK ACRES CINDERELLA
FC CROWDER
NFC MARTEN'S LITTLE SMOKEY
FC MARTEN'S LITTLE BULLET
CH. SHAMROCK ACRES EBONY LANCER
CH. WHYGIN GOLD BULLION
CH. WHYGIN GENTLE JULIA OF AVEC
Whygin Black Gambit of Avec
CH. SHAMROCK ACRES SOMEDAY SUE, C.D.
CH. SHAMROCK ACRES CASEY JONES, C.D.
CH. SHAMROCK ACRES LIGHT BRIGADE
CH. WHYGIN BUSY BELINDA
CH. SHAMROCK ACRES EARLY BIRD
AM. & CAN. CH. SHAMROCK ACRES SONIC BOOM
CH. SHAMROCK ACRES BLACK BUTTON
AM. & CAN. CH. WHYGIN CAMPAIGN PROMISE

Dr. and Mrs. John Ippensen
Sunnybrook Acres Kennel
Dr. Robert J. Berndt

Ch. Sunnybrook Acres Cinderella. Earl Graham Photography.

NFC and NAFC Super Chief.

DUAL CH. SHED OF ARDEN
DUAL CH. GRANGEMEAD PRECOCIOUS
Huron Lady
FC FREEHAVEN MUSCLES
FC HIWOOD MIKE
Grangemead Sharon
Grangemead Angel
FC & AFC PAHA SAPA CHIEF II
Good Hope Smoke
FC THE SPIDER OF KINGSWERE
Jean of Sandylands
Treasure State Be-Wise
NFC MARVADEL BLACK GUM
FC DEER CREEK BE-WISE
Symphony at Deer Creek
1967 NFC & 1967, 1968 NAFC SUPER CHIEF
DUAL CH. SHED OF ARDEN
DUAL CH. GRANGEMEAD PRECOCIOUS
Huron Lady
DUAL CH. CHEROKEE BUCK
FC HIWOOD MIKE
Grangemead Sharon
Grangemead Angel
Ironwood Cherokee Chica
Costal Charger of Deer Creek
NFC & NAFC CORK OF OAKWOOD LANE
Akona Liza Jane of Kingdale
Glen Water Fantom
NFC MARVADEL BLACK GUM
Little Peggy Black Gum
Comay Classy Chassis

August and Louise Belmont

CH. TORQUAY SCORPIO
CH. KILLINGWORTH THUNDERSON
Killingworth snipe
CAN. CH. FORECAST LYZ OF TRIPLE L
CH. BLACKMOR'S BUCKLIE
Forecast Aldelphi
Mallow's Fanfare
AM. CAN. CH. CHRISTY'S CASEY OF TRIPLE L CD WC
CH. SHAMROCK ACRES SONIC BOOM
CH. COULD BE'S BLACK ANGUS
CH. GARMERETTE OF CHARLOW
Teal Lakes Spun Gold
CH. SHAMROCK ACRES LIGHT BRIGADE
Shamrock Acres Carrousal
Shamrock Acres Bridget CD
AM. CAN. CH. TRIPLE L'S DAVEY CROCKETT WC
ENG. AM. CH. SANDYLANDS MIDAS
CH. TORQUAY SCORPIO
Mallow's Fancy Free
CH. KILLINGWORTH THUNDERSON
CH. ANNWYN'S JACK O'DIAMONDS
Killingworth Snipe
CH. WINDROW'S SAMANTHA
Triple L's Creme Rinse
CH. KIMVALLEY CLIPPA OF LAWNWOOD
AM. CAN. CH. JAGERSBO HOPE OF AQUARIUS
Jagersbo Black Pepper
AM. CAN. CH. JAGERSBO LYZ DINGALILNG THING
Jagersbo Yogi Bear
Jagersbo Wallaby
Jagersbo Yellow Gail

Carl and Jan Liepmann

Ch. Triple L's Davey Crocket.

Sam Duke of Randall
CH BRIARY BELL BOUY OF WINDSONG
CH. FOLLYTOWER SALLY
CH. WINDSONGS SILVER BULLET
CH. BRIARY BRENDAN OF RAINELL
WINDSONG'S MORNING MIST
Briary Maeve
CAN CH. TRIPLE L'S CORAL RIDGE
Forecast's Lzy of Triple L
CH. CHRISTY'S CASEY OF TRIPLE L
Teal Lakes Spun Gold
Triple L's Brite Sunnye Daze
CH. KILLINGWORTH'S THUNDERSON
Triple L's Cream Rinse
CH. JAGERSBO LZY DINGALING THING

Carl Liepmann

Ch. Triple L's Coral Ridge.

INT. & NOR. CH. BARONOR PHOENIX
INT. & NOR. CH. LICITHA'S BLIZZARD
NOR. CH. LICITHA'S POPPET
FIN. CH. KEITSUN UJO
ENG. CH. ELOWOOD SOUL SINGER
Priorise Secret
Priorise Mysterious
FIN. CH. SPENCEHILL'S BONDERA
FIN. CH. FAGELANGENS HAWKER HUNTER
FIN. CH. PASTIME'S SWING GATE
FIN. CH. PASTIME'S POUND CAKE
FIN. CH. MAILIKSEN FELINA
INT. & NOR. CH. LICITHA'S BLIZZARD
FIN. CH. ROSAUAU TASTE OF HONEY
Rosauau Jasmin

CH. TWEEDLEDOM WHITNEY DELIGHT
ENG. SH. CH. ARDMARGHA MAD HATTER
ENG. SH. CH. BRADKING CASSIDY
AM., CAN. & CAN. CH. BRADKING BLACK CHARM
ENG. CH. HEATHERBOURNE COURT JESTER
ENG. SH. CH. HEATHERBOURNE SILVER CZAR
ENG. SH. CH. COPPERHILL LYRIC OF HEATHERBOURNE
Copperhill Taffeta
Jayncourt Jingle Jangle
Sandylands Charlie Boy
Sandylands Charleston
ENG. SH. CH. SANDYLANDS LONGLEY COME RAIN
Jayncourt Peace
Jayncourt Rebel
Jayncourt Never Without
Zabadak of Jayncourt

Sharon and Philip E. Parr
Delight Labradors

Ch. Tweedledom Whitney Delight.

Ch. Venetian's Joyful Bridget. Bernard Kernan Photography.

Ballyduff Spruce
CH. CHARWAY BALLYWILL WILL
Charway Simona
AM. & CAN. CH. MERRYMILLS BUGLE BOY HEATHERBOURNE
ENG. SH. CH. BALRION KING FROST
Heatherbourne Fair Maiden
Heatherbourne Moira
CH. VENETIAN'S MIJAN DRUMMER BOY
ENG. CH. BALLYDUFF MARKETEER
CH. JAYNCOURT AJOCO JUSTICE
Jayncourt Star Performer
Mijans Natalia of Beechcroft
ENG. CH. TIMSPRING SIRIUS
CH. BALLY DUFF LARK
Spark of Ballyduff
CH. VENETIAN'S JOYFUL BRIDGET
Jayncourt Stormer
Waltham Galaxy of Condor
Waltham Lass
CH. MARBRA GUARDSMAN
ENG. CH. BALLYDUFF MARKETEER
Marbra Rhapsody
Marbra Palisander
CH. GLENLO'S CIDER
Anderscroft Stalyna Sioux
CH. MIJANS CORRIGAN
CH. DRIFTWOOD'S HONEYSUCKLE
CH. GLENLO'S VELVET REPLICA
Lockerbie Apollo
Glenlo's Velvet Tara
Venetian's Dolia Double Duck

Charlotte Veneziano
Venetian Labradors

DUAL CH. GRANGEMEAD PRECOCIOUS
FC FREEHAVEN MUSCLES
Grangemead Sharon
FC & AFC PAHA SAPA CHIEF II
FC & AFC THE SPIDER OF KINGWERE
Treasure State Be-Wise
FC DEER CREEK BE-WISE
NFC & NAFC SUPER CHIEF
DUAL CH. GRANGEMEAD PRECOCIOUS
DUAL CH. CHEROKEE BUCK
Grangemead Sharon
Ironwood Cherokee Chica
NFC & NAFC CORK OF OAKWOOD LANE
Glen Water Fantom
Little Peggy Black Gum
1974 NFC & 1976 NAFC & CNFC WANAPUM DART'S DANDY
Huron's Black Prince
Sambo of Somonnauk II
Duchess of Stonegate
Nettley Creeks Sugar
DUAL CH. BRACKEN SWEEP
Nelgard's Madam Queen
FC LADY'S DAY AT DEER CREEK
CAN. DUAL CH. DART OF NETTLEY CREEK
NFC MARVADEL BLACK GUM
Stonegate's Brazen Beau
Camay Classy Chassis
Stonegates Susie
DUAL CH. MATCHMAKER FOR DEER CREEK
Lucky Linda of Stonegate
Stonegate Char

Charles L. Hill

NFC. NAFC, and CNFC Wanapum Dart's Dandy.